Grow Great Marijuana

By

Logan Edwards

sweetleaf

Los Angeles, CA

Grow Great Marijuana

Published by
Sweetleaf Publishing
Los Angeles, CA

www.sweetleafpublishing.com

ISBN: 978-0-9776505-0-7

Printed in the United States of America

Cover and Interior Design: Chad Perry
Illustration: Ken
Editor: Chad Perry
Photography: Subcool, Paradise Seeds, T.H.Seeds

This book contains information about illegal substances, specifically the plant Cannabis Sativa and its derivative products. Sweetleaf Publishing would like to emphasize that cannabis is a controlled substance in North America and throughout much of the world. As such, the use and cultivation of cannabis can carry heavy penalties that may threaten an individual's liberty and livelihood.

The aim of the Publisher is to educate and entertain. Whatever the Publisher's view on the validity of current legislation, we do no in any way condone the use of prohibited substances.

Table of Contents

· ·

Introduction 1
   How to Use This Book...2
   How This Book Is Organized 3
      Part I: The Basics...3
      Part II: The Equipment 3
      Part III: The Grow 3
   Icons Used In This Book...4
   Now What? 5

Marijuana Basics 7
   The Marijuana Plant..8
      Males and Females 8
   How Marijuana Grows...9
      Trichomes and THC...9
      Varieties of Marijuana 9
         Sativa 10
         Indica 11
         Ruderalis...12
      How Marijuana Eats (Photosynthesis) 12
      How Marijuana Breathes (Respiration) 13
      How Marijuana Reproduces (Photoperiod)...........14
   Elements of Marijuana Growth...................................15
      Water 16
      Air..17
      Light 17
      Food 18
      Warmth..18
   Marijuana Cycle of Life..19
      Germination...20
      Seedling 21
      Vegetative Growth 21
      Preflowering 22
      Flowering 23
      Seed Set 24
      Conclusion 24

Hydroponic Basics **27**
Hydroponic Q & A 28
What's Wrong With Soil? 29
Hydroponics Pros and Cons 30
Advantages of Hydroponics 30
Disadvantages of Hydroponics 31

Where to Grow **33**
Choosing a Grow Room 34
Closets 35
Bedrooms 35
Basements 35
Attics 36
Planning for Plant Size 36
Growing Techniques 38
Sea of Green 38
Screen of Green 40
Using Advanced Techniques 41
Security Issues 41
Choosing the Right Spot 43
Planning Your Grow Room 44
Creating the Final Plan 48
Keeping Costs Down 50
Choosing Components 51

Lighting **53**
HID Lamps Explained 54
Types of Lighting Systems 57
High Pressure Sodium (HPS) 57
Enhanced Performance HPS 57
Metal Halide (MH) 58
Super Horizontal MH 58
Conversion Bulbs 58
Lighting Systems Components 60
Bulbs and Ballasts 61
Switchable ballasts 62
Bulb replacement 62
Reflectors 63
Horizontal reflectors 63

Vertical reflectors 63
Hoods 64
Air cooled 64
Dual fixture 64
HID Lighting Safety 65
Fluorescent Lighting 65
Fluorescent Bulb Color Spectrums 66
Reflective Wall Covering 67
Reflectance 67
Flat white paint...68
Mylar 68
Black and white poly...69
Aluminum foil 69
Mirrors 69
Cleaning Your Wall Covering 69
Seedling Lighting 70

Fans **89**
Why Airflow is Important? 90
Planning Air Movement 90
Air intake source 91
Oscillating fans 92
Exhaust fan and ducting 92
Creating an Air Intake Source 92
Vents 93
Creating an air intake vent..93
Intake Fans...93
Ducting...94
Oscillating Fans 95
Exhaust Fan and Ducting System 96
Choosing Your Fan Size...97
Installing your exhaust fan 97
Adjusting light timer cycles 98
Temperature..98
Hot Lamps...98
Measuring Temperature 99
Keeping the right temperature 100
Lowering grow room temperature..............................100
Raising grow room temperature.................................101

Humidity 102
   Lowering Humidity 103
   Humidity for Seedlings 103

Hydroponic Systems 105
Choosing a System 106
   Drip...106
   Ebb and Flow 107
   Aeroponic...109
   Nutrient Film Technique (NFT) 110
   Basic Components 111
System Maintenance...113
   Monthly Maintenance 114
   Post-Harvest Maintenance 114
Growing Medium...114
   Types of Medium 115
      Rockwool 115
      Clay pellets...117
      Coconut fiber..118
      Soilless mix 118
      Water culture 119
Managing the Medium..119

Water and Nutrients 121
Water Basics 122
   Water Quality 122
      Nutrient lockout repair 123
      Water temperature 124
pH Level Metering 124
   Types of Meters 126
      Waterproof pens 126
      Portable meters 126
      Constant monitoring meters...127
      pH test strips 127
      pH test kit..127
      Pen maintenance 128
      pH adjustment 128
Over Watering..129
Under Watering..129

Nutrient Basics 130
    Labeling Explained 132
        Preformulated nutrients 133
        Recommended nutrient brands...........................135
Nutrient Strength 136
    Overfeeding 137
    Nutrient Measurement...137
PPM Meters..138
Growing Medium Moisture 139
    Measuring Moisture Levels 139
Topping Off...139

Putting it all Together..143
    Preparing the Room 144
        Enclosing the Room 144
    Grounding your Electrical Equipment 145
        Electrical Safety Tips 145
    Hanging your Wall Covering.......................................146
    Protecting your Floor..147
    Placing your Circulation Fan 148
    Configuring Fans and Ducting....................................148
    Hanging Your Lights 149
        Horizontal Placement 150
        Vertical Placement 150

Grow Room Security 155
    Keep a Low Profile...156
    Buying Equipment Discreetly 157
        Dress and Act Appropriately................................157
            Clothes..157
            Car...158
            Attitude 158
        Paying for Equipment..158
            Do not use credit cards 159
            Do not shop online 159
        Moving Equipment Into Your Home 159
    Protecting Your Grow Room 159
        Don't Use a Burglar Alarm..................................160
        Padlock the Room..160

Stealth Trash Disposal 160
Odor Control..161
Ionizers 162
Ozone Generators..162
Placement 163
Maintenance 164
Activated Carbon Filters 164
Placement 165
Maintenance 166
Concealing your Grow Room......................................166
Light Leaks..166
Venting Hot Air..167
Fan Noise..168

Seeds and Seedlings 171
Acquiring Seeds..172
Varieties of Marijuana 172
Indicas..172
Sativas..172
Hybrids 173
Strain Characteristics 173
Outdoor or indoor 173
Height..173
Price and quality 174
Potency 174
Yield 175
Flowering times 175
Ten Great Strains to Get You Started....................176
Using Bag or Found Seeds 178
Choosing a Reputable Seed Bank................................179
Ordering Seeds 180
Money order 180
Cash..180
Credit card 181
Western Union...181
Seed Bank Problems 181
Seed Legalities 182
Seed Storage 182
Long Term Storage 182

Germination 183
    Easy Germination 183
    Direct Germination 184
Transplanting..184
    Equipment 185
        Heating pad 185
        One-inch rockwool or starter cubes.....................185
        Seedling tray 186
        Humidity dome 186
        Lighting..186
        Nutrients...186
    Step-by-Step Transplanting.................................187

Vegetative Growth **193**
    Nutrients..194
        Feeding Regiment 195
    Lighting...195
        Day Lengths 196
    Pruning...196
        Pruning Tips 197
            Over-pruning.....................................197
    Topping 197
    Thinning 199
    Training 200
    Advanced Techniques 202
        Twisting and Cracking................................202
        Splitting your Leaves.................................203
    Pre-Flower Identification 203
        Female Plants...203
        Male Plants...204
        Hermaphrodites 204
    Initiating Flowering..205

Clones and Mother Plants................................**225**
    Clone Potency...226
    Cloning to Determine Sex...................................226
    Mother Plants...227
        Choosing Mother Plants..............................228
        Desirable Characteristics 228

Cloning Equipment..229
Step by Step Cloning...231
    Clone Maintenance 237
    Checking for Roots..238
    Troubleshooting your Clones.........................240
Transplanting Clones...240
    Transplanting Into Flowering 241

Flowering 243

Nutrients...244
Lighting..244
    Light Type...245
Night Lengths 245
    Making it Dark 246
    Dark Period Accidents 246
Vegetative Growth While Flowering.....................246
Pruning Leaves While Flowering..........................247
Flushing the Medium 248
Determining Peak Harvest Time...........................249
    The Window of Harvest...............................249
    Head High or Body Stone? 250
    Determining Plant Maturity 250
    Magnify Your Buds 251
More about Trichomes..252

Harvesting 255

Getting ready to cut...256
    Gather Your Tools.......................................256
    Choosing a Cutting Spot 257
    Prepare Your Space......................................257
Cutting Down Your Plants 257
    Quick Cut...258
    Manicuring 259
        Cleaning 261
Drying Your Harvest 262
    Quick-Dry Methods....................................263
        Oven 264
        Microwave 264
        Ballast drying method............................264

Step-by-Step Curing 264
Watch for Mold 266
Ready to Smoke 266

Plant Stress and Pests.................................. 269
Plant Stress 270
Watering and Nutrients 270
Over watering 270
Low nutrient strength 271
Nutrient deficiencies 271
Root problems 271
Leaf Problems 272
Yellowing (Chlorosis)..............................272
Yellowing in lower to middle leaves 272
Yellowing in upper leaves (New Growth) 272
Leaf Curling 272
Stem Problems 273
Plant Diseases..273
Grey Mold (Botrytis) 274
Root Rot (Pythium) 274
Plant Pests 275
Domestic Pests...275
Spider Mites..276
Thrips 277
Whiteflies..278
Fungus Gnats 279

Index.. 281

Introduction

· ·

Welcome to *Grow Great Marijuana*! This book was written to serve a single purpose: to teach people how to grow great marijuana indoors. Based on my own experiences in learning how to grow, it's not as easy as it sounds. There is a lot of information already out there; some good, some bad, and some just too complicated to be useful.

When I started growing, I had always wished that there was a single book that taught the basics of how marijuana grows, what equipment I needed, and how to take care of and harvest the plants. Unfortunately, I had to read through a pile of books and make a lot of mistakes to get through my first few grows.

Some books I read were too technical, with a lot of detailed charts and diagrams. Other books were too simple and didn't answer the questions I needed answered. I was certain that all of the essentials could be put into one easy-to-read book that took the reader from the beginning to end of growing marijuana indoors.

And you? Maybe you've read through a few books and now have more questions than answers. Or maybe you don't know much about growing and want to find out if you could do it. Or maybe you've even tried to grow once or twice and just weren't happy with the results. In any case, this book was written with you in mind.

About This Book

If you've never grown marijuana before, you should read this book from cover to cover. You'll learn a lot, maybe more than you thought possible, about growing a single species of plant. For some, indoor growing will seem overwhelming and these pages will make for good use as rolling papers.

For most of you, this will be the beginning of a wonderful journey in producing some of greatest marijuana you have ever smoked. There is nothing more gratifying than packing bowls and smoking joints of great marijuana that you've nurtured from seed or clone to bountiful harvest.

Finally, some of you will become obsessed, not with marijuana itself, but with growing marijuana. Like a gear head is to a Camaro, you will constantly be on the lookout for ways to automate your grow room and increase your yields. It can be an expensive obsession, but everyone needs a hobby.

How to Use This Book

While this book was designed to be read cover-to-cover, you don't have to remember each and every detail or aspect of growing as you read through it. It's far better to get a basic understanding of how the plant grows naturally and what it's going to take to grow it indoors. Then, you can start designing your grow room and then put the pieces together one-by-one, chapter-by-chapter, learning what you need as you go along.

As a quick flip through this book will show you, technical charts and fancy diagrams are nowhere to be found. Instead, you'll find subjects like these, discussed in simple terms that naturally lead you from one section to the next:

✓ **Designing your room**

✓ **Buying the right equipment**

✓ **Securing your space**

✓ **Helping your plants grow**

✓ **Harvesting your buds**

How This Book Is Organized

The information in this book has been divided into three major parts covering the basics of how marijuana grows, the equipment you need to grow indoors, and how to use the equipment as your plants grow and bud. Each part contains chapters related to the part's theme. Chapters are divided into short sections to help you navigate and easily find what you're looking for.

Part I: The Basics

This book starts out with the basics. First, you find out how marijuana grows naturally in the outdoors, including the stages of growth and the simple processes that turn a tiny seed into a bud producing plant. It explains how hydroponics works and why people use it to grow plants. Finally, you will look at where you might grow and start thinking about the basic equipment you will need for the space.

Part II: The Equipment

If you grow outdoors using seeds, you can let mother nature handle most of the hard work. However, when growing indoors, *you* are responsible for recreating and providing everything your plants need to grow and flourish. In this part you will learn all of the ins and outs of what you need to get your plants up and growing. Instead of taking the technical approach, we'll break down each piece of equipment into just a few key decision points.

Part III: The Grow

Understanding how marijuana grows is the easy part. Buying all of the equipment is the expensive part. The grow is the most stressful part, but if you've read and followed the book up to this point, it's also the fun part. The Grow is where all of your planning and hard work pay off. Here, you learn how to take care of your plants through all of the growth phases until it's time to harvest.

Icons Used In This Book

There is a lot of information presented in this book and it's recommended that you read every bit of it, especially if you are new to growing Additionally, some key points are highlighted to emphasize their importance to both novice and experienced growers. Look for the icons below to help lead the way.

While most of the book provides comprehensive information on all of the important topics, sometimes a quick answer is all you need. If you see this icon, you'll find a simple answer to a question commonly asked by novice growers.

When you grow indoors using hydroponic systems, you have a lot of options in the types of products you can use to get the most out of your garden. This icon highlights how to use technology to get your plants growing to their greatest potential.

There is a lot of terminology associated with growing marijuana that even regular gardeners might not understand. Look for this icon to help explain what some of the more technical terms mean and how they apply to your plants and your grow room.

This icon alerts you to information about growing that will give you an extra edge in speeding your plants' growth rate, increasing yields, or providing extra security for your grow. If you've got the basics down, you will want to investigate these tips even further.

If you make a mistake with your indoor grow, the repercussions can be swift and deadly for your plants. Although marijuana is a resilient plant that can bounce back from stress and other problems, you will want to take extra precaution when you see this icon.

Now What?

Ready to grow? If you've never done it before, you should read this book cover to cover. If you have some experience, you might want to read the chapters that are important to you and skim the rest. Either way, this is *your* book, your guide to growing great marijuana. If you get confused or have questions, write them down in the book. Don't be afraid to circle sections that are relevant to your situation that you know you will have to come back to. The more you mark up the book, the easier it will be to find the information you need later on.

Chapter 1

Marijuana Basics

. . . .

In This Chapter

▶ How marijuana plants grow

▶ Understanding marijuana's cycle of life

▶ Getting to know how plants produce buds

▶ Exploring the different types of marijuana

. . . .

Marijuana basics can be understood most easily by keeping one simple fact in mind: cannabis is a plant, and a very highly evolved one at that. Plants are not designed to grow indoors, so in order to have a thriving indoor garden you must fool the plants into believing they're in the great outdoors. It's your job to mimic an outdoor environment by recreating the sun, the wind, the rainfall, and the climate conditions of an outdoor plot.

There are five major factors to plant growth: light, water, nutrients, atmosphere (oxygen and carbon dioxide), and temperature. Any green plant needs all five of these things to be available to it or growth will slow or stop. Each one is just as important as the others and more of one will absolutely not make up for lack of any other.

Each limiting factor is a link in the chain. The weak link is the one that slows the plants down. If you think you have a problem as you are growing, it's most likely one of the five factors.

The Marijuana Plant

The key to growing great marijuana is understanding how it uses just a few basic elements to produce food for growth and how it grows from a small seedling to mature plant. That should be the case with most any plant you hope to grow. Beyond those fundamentals, you also need to learn about how marijuana produces the natural chemicals known as cannabinoids, because ultimately that's what gets you "high."

First you need to learn that there are male and female marijuana plants and why destroying the males in your garden can eliminate seed production and increase the THC content in your females. Then you'll naturally want to find out what THC is and how it's produced. Finally, you should get to know the different varieties of marijuana as well as why there are so many strains.

Males and Females

Marijuana develops as a male (pollen producing), female (ovule producing), or occasionally hermaphroditic (containing both male and female parts) plant. As the male plant blooms it begins to develop pollen-producing flowers. In the outdoors, the wind usually blows this pollen onto the female flowers, culminating in fertilization.

After releasing its pollen, the male plant has completed its life cycle, so it wilts and dies. After a female plant becomes fertilized, it begins devoting its energy to creating a seed set, while it too begins to die. The mature seeds are then left on the ground to germinate and perpetuate the combined genetic traits of both male and female, father and mother.

This is the natural method that allows marijuana to grow on and on in rural fields and backwater ditches. By understanding the basics of how marijuana reproduces and by using the indoor hydroponic method, you will be able to easily spot and remove males, if you desire, before they fully develop flowers. This eliminates the possibility of the females becoming fertilized and producing a seed set which allows them to concentrate on developing that sticky resin known at THC.

How Marijuana Grows

Trichomes and THC

When a marijuana plant flowers, it begins to produce sticky resin glands on leaves and buds; these glands, in the form of trichomes, contain most of the plant's THC (Tetrahydrocannabinol). Females produce the most resin to protect her and her seed set from the harsh outdoor environment. Males also produce THC, but in very low quantities. Why the trichomes contain psychoactive compounds is still a matter of evolutionary debate.

While THC is what you're after, it's the actual trichomes that you're looking for. From a distance, these tiny glandular stalks are difficult to identify, but by using a inexpensive microscope, you'll be able to observe their development before and after harvesting the plant. The trichomes are also largely responsible for the individual aroma of the plant.

There is a lot of technical information on how THC affects the brain, the various types of cannabinoids, and the different forms of trichomes. Each can be its own discipline, but none are very relevant to growing good marijuana. As long as you use high quality seeds, provide your plants with all of the elements they need, and properly harvest your crop, you will be rewarded with great marijuana.

Varieties of Marijuana

Technically speaking, there is only one species of marijuana, *Cannabis sativa*. By technically speaking, I mean that all marijuana plants are scientifically and legally classified as *Cannabis sativa* even though every grower acknowledges that there are three different "varieties" of marijuana within the species.

If that's not confusing enough, there are literally thousands of different genetic strains, each with a different high, flavor, fragrance, THC content, flowering time, and a host of other traits. Nowadays you can search a web site or flip through a catalogue and find hundreds of exotic strains, most of which you could be growing in a matter of weeks.

The two main varieties of marijuana are Indica and Sativa and there are many strains that are crosses of these two varieties. Within each variety, there are a huge number of individual strains, each with a different taste, aroma, and high.

Sativa

Sativa plants are characterized by spiky leaves and long thin flowers that are light green in color. This variety grows very quickly and can reach heights of twenty feet in a single season. Sativa's higher THC to CBD ratio produces a cerebral, soaring type of high that's more energetic, which can stimulate brain activity and may produce hallucinations.

Figure 1-1:
Typical Sativa leaf and Sativa plant outline.

Sativas originate from equatorial regions such as Colombia, Mexico, Thailand and Southeast Asia, where the growing season is warmer. Because of this, they are not generally used for outdoor cultivation in colder climates, although some hybrids can produce good yields under these conditions.

Once flowering has begun, Sativas can take anywhere from 10 to 16 weeks to fully mature. They contain less chlorophyll and more accessory pigments (protection from excessive sunlight) than Indicas. Because of this, Sativas take longer to grow, mature, and require more light. They tend to grow taller and more gangly than Indicas, which produces a lower, but more potent, yield. In general, pure Sativas are best suited for outdoor growing.

Indica

Indica plants are characterized by broad, short leaves and heavy, tight flowers. Indica buds are usually thick and dense, with flavors and aromas ranging from pungent skunk to sweet and fruity. The smoke from an Indica is generally a body-type stone, relaxing and laid back. Indica's higher CBD than THC ratio produces a much heavier, sleepy type of high. Indica plants have a heavy, stony high that is relaxing and it's effects are preferred by medicinal users.

Figure 1-2:
Typical Indica leaf and Indica plant outline.

Indicas originally come from the hash producing countries of the world like Afghanistan, Morocco, and Tibet, where the weather varies and growing conditions can be harsh. Because of the adaptability to many climates, Indica strains are ideal for indoor and outdoor cultivation in cooler climates.

Once flowering has begun, Indicas usually take six to eight weeks to mature. They contain more chlorophyll and less accessory pigments than Sativas. Because of this, Indicas grow faster than Sativas, which shortens the season and decreases the amount of space required. In general, Indicas and Indica/Sativa hybrids are recommended for growing indoors because you can harvest more often in a small environment.

Ruderalis

Ruderalis plants grow wild in parts of Eastern Europe and Russia are their seeds are difficult to find commercially. They are characterized by their early flowering, with some plants starting based how long they have been growing, rather than their photoperiod.

Figure 1-3:
Typical
Ruderalis
leaf and
Ruderalis
plant
outline.

Ruderalis is ideal for cultivation in cooler climates and areas where conditions are harsh. They are not recommended for indoor growing, mainly because they are difficult to force flower and their flowering times vary wildly. The results in yield and intensity can be unpredictable, which is the main reason why they are not available through seed banks.

How Marijuana Grows

How marijuana, or any plant, grows and reproduces is a complex subject, but for our purposes it doesn't have to be. You're simply growing a plant, albeit in a ultra-efficient, secure, indoor environment. Consider the following just a refresher on what marijuana has to do on the inside to produce what you love on the outside.

How Marijuana Eats (Photosynthesis)

Plants use light (like the Sun or a lamp) by channeling its energy into the formation of chemical bonds. The harvesting of light leads to a series of events in which water, CO_2, and light energy are used to create simple molecules called carbohydrates. The carbohydrates are used as stored energy that can later be used, in conjunction with nutrients (nitrogen, sulfur, phosphorus, etc.) drawn through the roots, to construct other molecules needed for plant growth. The large-scale process of converting light into energy-rich food molecules, called photosynthesis, is a function unique to plant life.

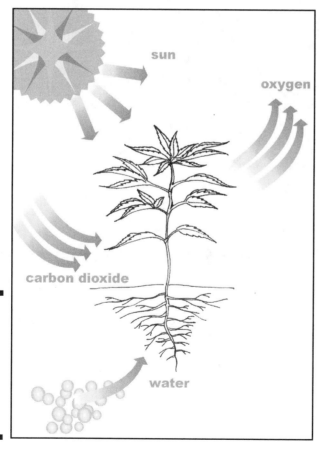

Figure 1-4:
Plants
use light
energy and
nutrients
to grow,
respiring
oxygen as
waste.

How Marijuana Breathes (Respiration)

In a way, respiration is the opposite cycle of photosynthesis. Respiration is the process by which plants break down the carbohydrates created during photosynthesis and release energy that can be used as food to continue its life processes, such as building and repairing cells and fighting disease. Technically, plants do not need light to carry out the respiration process, but respiration would not be possible without photosynthesis, a process plants most certainly need light to perform.

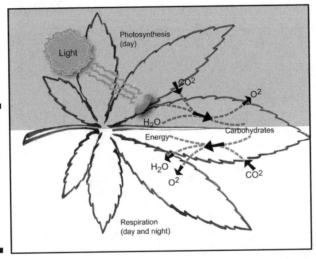

Figure 1-5:
Plants use light energy and nutrients to grow, respiring oxygen as waste.

How Marijuana Reproduces (Photoperiod)

In addition to light being the catalyst for carbohydrate production in plants, light or more specifically the length of time light is absent, otherwise know as a plant's dark period, determines when a plant begins to flower or bud, which ultimately initiates reproduction. This is what is known as a plant's photoperiod.

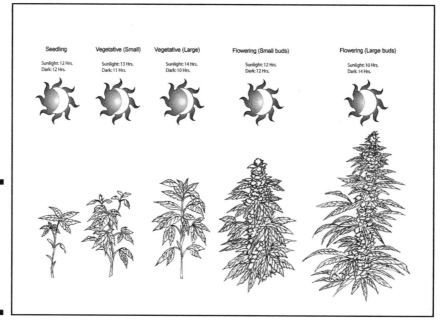

Seedling | Vegetative (Small) | Vegetative (Large) | Flowering (Small buds) | Flowering (Large buds)

Sunlight: 12 Hrs.
Dark: 12 Hrs.

Sunlight: 13 Hrs.
Dark: 11 Hrs.

Sunlight: 14 Hrs.
Dark: 10 Hrs.

Sunlight: 12 Hrs.
Dark: 12 Hrs.

Sunlight: 10 Hrs.
Dark: 14 Hrs.

Figure 1-6:
The amount
of darkness
a plant
receives
determines
its growth
phase.

A plant's photoperiod is the response in the plant to the changing lengths of
day and night. The cannabis plant's initiation of flowering is the process most
frequently associated with changing the plant's light cycle from 18-24 hours
of light per day to 12 hours of light per day in a 24-hour period.

Elements of Marijuana Growth

Like most living things, a plant needs water, air, light, food, and warmth. These
are the essential elements required to grow almost any type of plant, not just
marijuana. Take any one of these away and your plants won't grow very well. Let's
take a look at each of these factors so you can start to understand what you'll have
to provide for your plants when growing indoors.

Figure 1-7:
Each factor
is crucial
to plant
growth.
Abundance
of one does
not make up
for the lack
of another.

Water

About 80% of a living plant's weight is water. Besides being used as a transportation-medium, the majority of the water absorbed by the roots will be used to keep a plant cool. This works the same as with human beings; by evaporating water, heat is dissipated, which results in a cooler body. The rest of the water is used in the plant's photosynthesis process. Photosynthesis is a complicated process where the plant builds carbohydrates from water, nutrients, CO_2, and light-energy. These carbohydrates are later combined with other chemical compounds absorbed from air and soil and transformed into new plant growth.

Air

It seems that everybody understands the importance of light and water in the process of photosynthesis. But another factor, carbon dioxide (CO_2), is always underestimated.

The CO_2 formula tells us that carbon dioxide is a molecule made of one carbon and two oxygen atoms. The carbon atom is of importance here because oxygen is just waste, at least to the plants. There is only one carbon atom in each molecule of CO_2 and there is only about 0.3% CO_2 in normal air, which isn't much. Because of this, it is important that marijuana plants have a constant supply of fresh air.

Light

Light energy is used to form carbohydrates like sugar, starch and cellulose that are used by the plant to build and repair plant tissue. Of course this can only take place if there is a source of light available. The light we see from the sun is a mix of all colors. Plants use mainly blue and red light, depending on which growth phase they are in.

Since you plan to grow indoors, where the sun refuses to shine, you have to use another light source. One problem with using artificial lights is that normal bulbs don't give enough light for a plant to thrive and they emit light in the wrong colors. The only types of light bulbs able to provide enough light for plants to grow properly and in the right color spectrum are Metal Halide (MH) bulbs for vegetative growth and High-Pressure Sodium (HPS) bulbs for flowering. These bulbs are used in High Intensity Discharge (HID) lighting systems, which are capable of giving plants the powerful illumination they require.

For the vegetative (growing) phase of a plant's life cycle you need more of the cool, blue light that MH bulbs provide. If you are just growing seedlings, you could also use fluorescent lighting, but that's an entirely different discussion. Marijuana that is in the flowering (budding) phase needs more of the orange-red light provided by HPS bulbs.

Food

Okay, we have light, water, and air, now it's time to eat. When humans eat, our meal is digested in our stomach, another weird chemical process involving things you may not want to know about. Our cells can't do anything with, let's say, a piece of banana, so it's ripped apart into smaller elements which our bodies' cells can use for growth and other processes. Among other things, acid is used to split complex molecules into easier-to-handle smaller molecules and elements.

A similar "elemental breakdown" applies to marijuana plants as well. Plants can't nourish on the complex molecules found in the medium at which they root, be it soil or any artificial medium. Plants are not equipped with a stomach, so they are in a bit of a disadvantage. Plants have to pre-digest their food, so to speak, by using CO_2 and light energy. Through photosynthesis, they are able to break down their nutrients into elements that they can use to grow, repair, and eventually flowering and produce seeds.

Warmth

And finally, since eating and growing means work and all work costs energy, this is where warmth becomes important. If a certain temperature is not reached, growth will happen at a slower rate or if it's really cold, there will be no growth at all. Maintaining a certain range in temperate is especially true for roots, which should be kept about ten degrees cooler than the air around your plants.

Conclusion

Water, air, light, food, and warmth are all essential growing factors. They all have to be in provided for or you will find that your plants won't grow as well as they could. Remember that you can't make up for the lack of one factor by overcompensating with another. If fact, this could harm your plants even more. More nutrients or watering will not make up for weak lighting. More lighting will never make up for lack of ventilation. All of these factors must be accounted for or you will never grow great marijuana.

Next, you will learn about how the marijuana plant uses these five factors to complete it's cycle of life.

Marijuana Cycle of Life

Cannabis is an annual plant, so in a single season (four to nine months) it completes it's life cycle. The precise length of the life cycle is dependant on the plant's variety, but is also regulated by local growing conditions, specifically the photoperiod (length of day vs. night). Cannabis is a long night (or short day) plant. When exposed to a period of two weeks of long nights (12 hours or more of continuous darkness each night), the plants respond by flowering.

This has important implications, for it allows the grower to control the life cycle of the plant and adapt it to local growing conditions. Since you can control flowering, you can control maturation and, hence, the age of the plants at harvest. Other than for security, the ability to force flower marijuana is the main reason why indoor growing has become so popular.

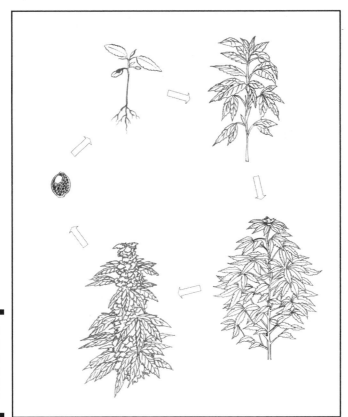

Figure 1-8: The cannabis plant's "cycle of life."

The following sections describe each phase of the marijuana plant's natural cycle of life. If your plants were growing outdoors, they would most likely follow each phase of the cycle. Since you plan to grow indoors, you have the ability to speed up some parts, such as the vegetative phase, and eliminate some parts altogether, such as germination (through cloning mother plants) and seed set (through "sexing" your plants).

Germination

After the coldness of winter subsides, spring air begins to warm, stirring activity in the embryo of the seed. As water is absorbed, the embryo's tissues swell, splitting the seed along its edge. The embryonic root appears, sheds the shell of the seed, then begins its downward growth.

As the roots grow and take hold in the ground, the top of the germinated seed begins to grow its stem upwards. Once the roots anchor themselves in the ground and begin receiving water and nutrients, the embryonic leaves, also known as cotyledons, unfold. The cotyledons are a pair of small, oval leaves that turn green with chlorophyll and help absorb the light energy to keep the plant growing. The process of germination usually take between three and ten days.

Figure 1-9: The embryo naturally grows towards the source of warmth and light.

Seedling

The formation of the second pair of leaves begins the seedling stage. The second set develop opposite of each other and usually have just one blade. They differ from the cotyledons by their larger size, spearhead shape, and serrated edges. The third set of leaves usually have usually have three blades and are larger than second set.

As the seedling develops more and more sets of new leaves, each set is larger than the last and has a higher number of leaves per blade until, depending on variety, they reach their maximum number. This is usually seven leaves per blade, but may be as many as nine or eleven leaves. The seedling stage is complete when the plant has reached this maximum leaves per blade, usually within four to six weeks.

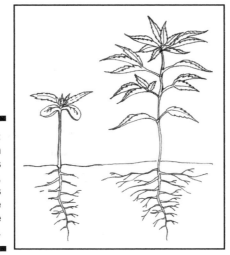

Figure 1-10:
When branches alternate, the plant has entered the vegetative phase.

Vegetative Growth

The vegetative phase is the plant's period of maximum growth. The plant grows only as fast as its leaves allow by collecting solar energy and producing the building blocks required for new growth. As the plant develops more leaf tissue, the plant increases its capacity for growth. With optimal growing conditions, Cannabis can grow as much as six inches a day, although the rate is usually closer to one or two inches.

The number of blades on each leaf decreases around the middle of the vegetative growth phase. Then, the alignment of leaves on the stem changes from being opposite of each other to alternate of each other. The internodes (stem spaces between sets of leaves, which had been increasing in length) begins to decrease and the growth appears to be thicker. The natural vegetative phase is usually completed in the third to fifth month of growth.

Figure 1-11:
The vegetative phase determines the eventual yield.

Preflowering

When a plant begins to preflower, for a quiet period of one to two weeks, growth begins to dramatically slow down. The plant begins to divert its energy from green growth to seed production as is encoded in its genes.

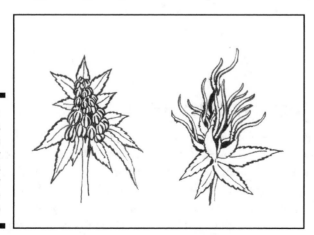

Figure 1-12:
Preflowers help you indentify males before they pollinate your crop

Flowering

Cannabis is dioecious, meaning each plant produces either male or female flowers and is considered either a male or female plant.

Male plants usually start to develop flowers about one month before females. First the upper internodes elongate and a few days later, male flowers start appearing. The male flowers are pale green or red/purple in color and appear as tiny balls hanging from the plant. These balls develop in dense clusters that release clouds of pollen dust. Once pollen falls, the males lose vigor and begin to die.

Female flowers consist of two small, fuzzy white stigmas attached at the base to an ovule which is formed from modified leaves that surround the developing seed. Female flowers develop tightly together to form dense clusters or buds. The flowers continue to bloom until pollen fertilizes them and they begin producing seeds. Flowering usually lasts about two months, but may take longer depending on the plant's strain, if it has been pollinated, and if the weather is unseasonably mild.

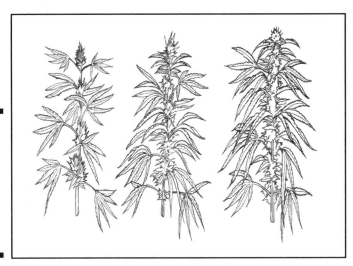

Figure 1-13: As the light cycle changes, the plant devotes energy towards bud production.

Seed Set

A fertilized female flower develops a single seed, wrapped in bracts. In thick clusters, they form the seed-filled buds that make up most fine imported marijuana. After pollination, mature viable seeds take from ten days to five weeks to develop. When seeds are desired, the plant is harvested when enough seeds have reached full color. For a fully seeded plant, this often takes place when the plant has stopped growth and is, in fact, dying.

Conclusion

Now that you've read about the basics of marijuana, you should know how marijuana grows, what your plants need in order to grow, and the cycle of life in which they grow. The next chapter gives you the basics on how indoor hydroponics can be used to harvest up to six marijuana crops every year!

Chapter 2

Hydroponic Basics

- -

In This Chapter

▶ Common questions about hydroponics

▶ Advantages to using the hydroponic technique

▶ Drawbacks of hydroponic growing

- -

The word hydroponic is derived from the Greek words hydro (water) and ponos (labor), meaning water working. The modern definition of hydroponics is the science of growing plants without soil by using an inert medium such as coconut fiber, water, peat, Vermiculite, Perlite, Rockwool, and many others. Soil is not needed because a nutrient solution is supplied to the plants and contains all the essential elements needed for normal growth and development.

Hydroponic crops can be grown indoors or in outdoor beds. Most often, hydroponic growers use beds, troughs, tanks, or bags inside a controlled environment like a closet or spare room. This controlled environment allows the grower immense control over the performance of their marijuana plants. Crop production and quality is highest with optimum levels of light, temperature, humidity and CO_2 (carbon dioxide). Nutrients are supplied to the growing plants in a nutrient solution that is pumped or drip-irrigated around the roots.

Hydroponic Q & A

People interested in growing indoors are often intimidated by the word
"hydroponics." The word itself sounds technical, complex, and expensive,
but for the purposes of growing a small number of plants in a closet
or basement, it really isn't. The following are some basic questions and
misconceptions about what hydroponics is and how regular, everyday
people can use it to their benefit.

Is hydroponics a new technology?

Hydroponics is not a "new" technology, it is has been in general use
for thousands of years. The Pharaohs of Ancient Egypt enjoyed fruits
and vegetables grown hydroponically. One of the Seven Wonders of
the World, The Hanging Gardens, was in fact a hydroponic garden.
Hydroponics is not new, just different.

Are hydroponic systems unnatural?

Plant growth is a real and natural occurrence. Plants require basic,
natural things for normal growth. Simply put, hydroponics supplies
the plant with what it needs, when it needs it. There is no genetic
mutation that takes place inside the equipment, nor are there any
mysterious chemicals given to the plants' roots that trick them into
thinking they're on steroids.

Is hydroponic growing harmful to the environment?

Growing plants hydroponically is far more "earth friendly" than
conventional gardening could ever be. Hydroponic water usage is
70 to 90 percent less then that used in conventional dirt gardening
and no fertilizer is lost to rain run off. These two items alone, water
conservation and the non-pollution of lakes and streams, are major
incentives to using hydroponics.

Is hydroponic growing expensive?

You may have seen hydroponics on display at a state fair or at a certain
Orlando theme park. These systems are on the cutting edge of modern
technology. The scientists there are researching ways to grow huge amounts

of food in the extreme conditions found on barren waste lands, deserts and even in outer space. Smaller systems, practical and easily affordable, that utilize the exact same principles and work just as well, are available today for the average hobby gardener at relatively inexpensive prices.

Does growing hydroponically produce superior plant growth?

Hydroponics *can* produce superior plant growth and superior yields in contrast to unpredictable outdoor growing conditions. Every seed, seedling and plant has a genetic ability to grow at a certain rate, to yield a certain amount of bud and for that bud to smoke and taste a certain way. All of these characteristics are controlled by a plant's genetic make-up and there isn't anything anyone can do that will make the plant exceed its natural genetic limits.

Getting a plant to grow to its full potential in common soil is difficult because of the hundreds of variables in the soil's make-up that influence the plant and its growth. It is the ability to control these variables that makes hydroponics superior to conventional gardening. You have full control over what the plant has available to it rather than guessing what the soil can provide. Because of this, the plants can display growth superior to plants grown in soil, but can only grow according to its inherited genetic capability.

What's Wrong With Soil?

In soil, biological decomposition breaks down organic matter into the basic nutrient salts that plants feed on. Water dissolves these salts and allows uptake by the roots. For a plant to receive a well balanced diet, everything in the soil must be in perfect balance. Rarely, if ever, can you find such ideal conditions in soil due to contamination and biological imbalances.

With hydroponics, water is enriched with these very same nutrient salts, but the hydroponic nutrient solution is contained. Hydroponics solution doesn't harm our environment, as does runoff from fertilized soil. Additionally, very little water is lost to evaporation in a hydroponic system.

Beyond all the technical benefits of using a hydroponic medium, soil can be extremely messy to work with, especially indoors.

Hydroponics Pros and Cons

Now that we've dispelled a few of the common myths about hydroponics, you should also be aware of the major benefits of using this fantastic growing technology as well as some of the drawbacks.

Advantages of Hydroponics

There are a number of advantages when using hydroponic production systems. Most importantly, hydroponics makes it possible to produce high quality marijuana in locations where it couldn't normally be grown in soil. In addition, hydroponics can increase product quality and makes more efficient use of resources such as space, water and plant nutrients.

- Hydroponic production often allows higher crop yields from smaller areas. Plant density is limited only by available light under controlled conditions.
- Plants can mature faster and more evenly under a soilless hydroponics system than under soil production. You can harvest some strains of marijuana up to six times per year under the most ideal conditions.
- Soil-borne insect and disease problems are reduced under soilless production systems.
- There are usually less or no pesticide applications when using hydroponic growing systems. Outdoor growers must rely on herbicides, fungicides and/or insecticides for optimum production.
- Nutrient application timing (watering) and nutrient quantities (strength) can be custom-tailored to the marijuana plant's specific needs. Nutrient release timing is much more difficult than outdoor growing.
- Hydroponic systems often make more efficient use of water and fertilizers than outdoor grows. Also, water stress is normally not a problem for hydroponic systems, if monitored properly.

Disadvantages of Hydroponics

While the list of advantages is long, hydroponics is not without its problems. It has a place to fill special needs, but is still a long way from replacing traditional soil-based methods.

⚘ Cost is a major concern. The initial investment required to set up some systems is much higher than soil-based production. Specialized equipment is often necessary for hydroponics. It also can be costly to operate and maintain hydroponic systems.

⚘ More skill is required than for traditional methods. The grower/operator must be knowledgeable about plant nutrition and system operation. Complex plant nutritional problems may arise during production. The growing system needs to be closely monitored for plant nutrient stress and water stress, either of which can affect crop growth.

⚘ Sanitation is extremely important, especially with indoor hydroponic environments. Water-borne plant diseases can spread quickly through some methods of hydroponic production.

Chapter 3

Where to Grow

In This Chapter

▶ Choosing the right grow space

▶ Getting to know the equipment for your room

▶ Creating a plan for your grow room

▶ Keeping costs down

Whether your intended growing area is a basement, a closet, a bathroom, an entire room, or any space in between, an indoor grow room allows you great influence over how well your plants can grow. With the right planning, preparation, and execution, you can use your grow room to harvest your own tasty buds three, four, and even five times more often than Earth's seasonal nature allows.

The best grow rooms usually begin with a well thought-out plan. Most indoor growers benefit by carefully designing their grow room and writing their plans down on paper. Many factors determine the size and quality of your harvest and these must be weighed against other factors such as how much time you can devote to the project, how much money you are willing to spend, how large of a grow space you have access to, and how secure you want your harvest to be.

This chapter will provide you with enough information to figure out where you can construct your grow room, how much cannabis you can realistically grow there, and what you will need to spend to accomplish this. Your grow room can be a major investment of time and money and if you're serious about growing, it most likely will be.

Choosing a Grow Room

Marijuana is grown in all kinds of places: perfectly built greenhouses, closets, basements or spare bedrooms. Every place has its advantages and drawbacks, but some simple guidelines should be followed when choosing a space.

🌿 **You don't want any light to enter or leave the room.**
The brightness, but especially the color of the lamps used, can draw attention from your neighbors. From the plants point of view, it's even more important that no light gets in. The hormones that trigger the process of flowering are initiated by twelve solid hours of darkness. Only if the plants are kept in total darkness for twelve hours per day will this hormone be able to initiate flowering.

🌿 **You want air to get in and out as much as possible.**
Ventilation fans and some ducting may be required to expel stagnant air and replace it with fresh (CO_2-rich) air that the plants use for growth. When trying to pick out a space, visualize how you will provide fresh air to the room and how you will get rid of the stale air.

🌿 **You need access to fresh water.**
A nearby tap makes life a lot easier because growing marijuana uses a lot of water. Since growing hydroponically means you have to flush the growing media on a regular basis, a way to get rid of the waste-water also comes in very handy. You should select a room that could be supplied with water by a reasonably-sized garden hose.

🌿 **You need electricity that is grounded to the earth.**
Most grow rooms have electrical sockets nearby, but for those who don't, you will have to use heavy-duty extension cords to bring the electricity to the room. If the room is anywhere near unfriendly foot traffic, the cords must be discreet and undetectable.

🌿 **You need a space that is secure.**
Most importantly, you need a grow space that cannot be easily detected or discovered. Review the complete list of security issues in this chapter to learn what to look for in a secure grow room. Also, read the Safety and Security chapter for information on how to protect your grow room from cops, visitors, and nosy neighbors.

Now that you know about the features that you should look for in a good grow room, let's have a look at the drawbacks and advantages of specific spaces.

Closets

For most people, a spare closet is the most obvious choice to use as a grow room. Closets are built to inherently conceal whatever may be inside them, although additional security measures will need to be taken. Closets are also self-contained, which makes it easier to control the atmosphere, including getting air in and out.

Closets *do* have their drawbacks though. Heat build-up can easily become a problem without proper ventilation. Electrical cords will most likely need to be fed into the closet and light can leak in and out through the door cracks. Also remember that you need room to work in your garden, so if the space is small or cramped with closet junk, it could be difficult to work in. Despite these drawbacks, a closet may be your only option. If it's a large or walk-in closet, it may be your best option.

Bedrooms

Bedrooms offer good opportunities, but temperature can be a bit of a problem. On the other hand, most of the time it's simple to adjust the room to your plants' needs because walls and ceiling are flat and straight-cornered. However, there may still be some constructing to do to create false walls to partition part of the room for growing.

One challenge could be the windows that have to be sealed off so that no light can get in or out. Simply nailing them shut with plywood could attract unwanted attention, so at least hang up a nice curtain before nailing a board up. Windows could be used to get fresh air into the room, but you wouldn't want to use them to get stale air out because you don't know who might be outside smelling the sweet bouquet of your marijuana plants. Also, strong winds might blow the air in, consequently impeding your ventilation from working properly.

Basements

Most of the time, basements will have a constant temperature and humidity, which makes controlling the atmosphere very easy. Getting enough air in and out, as well as getting rid of water, could be a problem. If you have a chimney or something similar to get rid of the exhaust-air, a basement would be near perfect.

Attics

The main problem with attics is the temperature. In the summer it may get too hot and in winter your plants may get too cold. Reversing the light cycle so that the light turns on at night and turns off during the day sometimes alleviates this problem. Another problem with some attics is that they are just not large enough to hang lamps properly and can be too cramped to work in. Attics come in many shapes and sizes, so it's up to you to determine what you can and can't do in your space.

Planning for Plant Size

The amount of space you have dictates how many plants you can grow and how many lights you can use, which ultimately determines how large a yield is possible. Having a very large grow space without enough light to spur rapid growth is not ideal. Overcrowding a small space with too many plants is also a mistake that will lead to a less than optimum yield.

To put it simply, plant growth is powered by light. In essence, they "eat" light. So your harvest doesn't solely depend on how many plants you have or how large of a space you have to put them in, but how much light is available. The only thing you can't have too much of is light.

For example, let's say you have two grow rooms, one room is 3' x 4' (12 sq/ft) and holds twelve plants. The other room is 4' x 6' (24 sq/ft) and holds twenty-four plants. Both of these rooms use a 600-watt HPS lighting system hanging from the middle of the room. You might think you would get a bigger yield from the larger grow room containing more plants, right?

Wrong! You would get the same or possibly even a smaller harvest from the larger room. Available lighting largely determines your eventual harvest if all other factors are optimum. As you will learn in the lighting chapter, the further the distance the plant is from the light source, the exponentially less light it will receive.

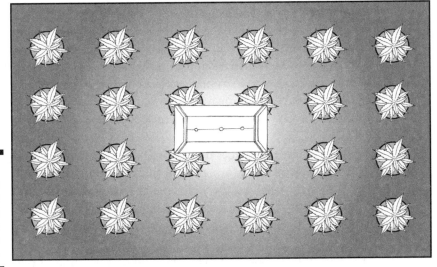

Figure 3-1:
A large grow space requires a lot of light to ensure even growth.

The twelve plants in the smaller room have access to just as much light, but spread over a smaller space and thus more intense. The plants on the edges of the larger 24-plant room receive inadequate light and produce inferior buds and take light away from the plants directly under the light.

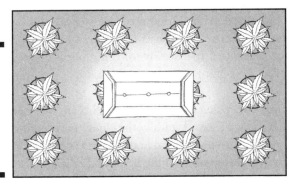

Figure 3-2:
Smaller grow room can yield large amounts with intense lighting.

Growing Techniques

If you happen to be working with a small room or you just want to maximize your yield in a small space, you have a few options beyond the simple "one plant per square foot" guideline. Beyond the basics of growing indoors with lights, some growers have taken their technique to the next level because of security concerns or to maximize production in small areas. While there are many variations on how to grow indoors, the Sea of Green (SOG) and Screen of Green (ScrOG) techniques have emerged as the most popular.

Although these techniques diverge from the usual methods of indoor growing, most of the information in this book can be applied to either one. Just make sure that the strain you grow is appropriate for these "short growth" techniques. Some strains have even been bred to thrive specifically under SOG and ScrOG growing techniques.

The type of hydroponics system you build or buy can limit the success of these techniques. If you are buying a commercial system, use internet discussion boards to see if anyone else has had success using the system with SOG or ScrOG. Some systems place plants too far apart for these techniques to be worthwhile or effective, while others have been specifically designed for them. Make sure you know *before* you buy.

Sea of Green

The Sea of Green method was developed to maximize the number of harvests grown in limited height situations. In a typical SOG setup, clones are planted at densities as high as four plants per square foot. Strains have been developed specifically for this environment, so they grow bushier, rather than fight upward for the light.

Within a short time after being established, the lights are switched to a twelve hour dark period to flower them. Typically, the clones have a growth spurt, forming a woody main stem and several branches. If the plant is suitable for SOG growing, it will stop short of the lights and fully bud. Most Indica strains are ideal for this method because their growth levels off after two weeks of flowering, followed by harvest six weeks later. The quick turnover from vegetative growth to flowering is the heart of the SOG method, as it results in the shortest possible plant flowering in the quickest possible time.

Since the plants were kept short, they each maintain one large bud that gets the maximum amount of light at the top. Most of the plants' growth energy is devoted to the top instead of the lower to middle branches. Growers using this technique are most interested in getting the largest harvest, with the most potent buds, using a very small grow space in the shortest amount of time.

Originally this technique was used with small-powered (under 400-watt) lamps and a limited number of plants. Eventually growers started using very powerful lamps and large tables filled with plants. Because of this, cloning becomes a major concern.

If you plan to use the method, be prepared to learn all about cloning, because it's vital to maintaining a perpetual harvest with so many small plants. Generally, your clones are grown vegetatively for only a week or two and then immediately sent into the SOG "flowering chamber" to keep them small. Within six to eight weeks, the plants are ready to be harvested and replaced with new clones.

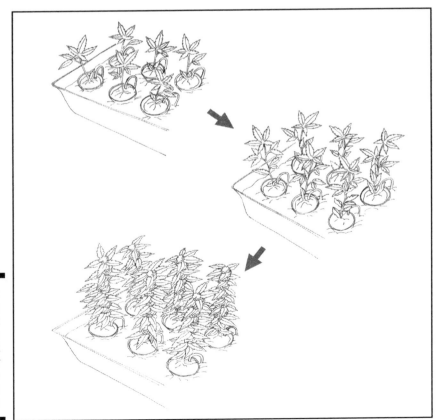

Figure 3-3:
Growing plants at a uniform height ensures your plants get the same lighting intensity.

Screen of Green

In its most simple form, the Screen of Green technique involves using a large mesh screen, usually poultry netting, and suspending it between the growing medium and the lamp. The plants grow up to the screen and then are "trained" to grow along the length of the screen, rather than straight through. This results in a flat "table" of plant growth, a field rather than a forest.

Because most of the plant shoots are grown at the same height (against the screen), your plant growth is equally exposed to the circle of light above, maximizing production from the space. Instead of having a few great buds at the top, some decent buds in the middle, and some airy, low-potency buds near the bottom, all of the buds at screen-level grow like plant tops. This method can be very effective with practice and can decrease the number of plants you have to grow, which may be desirable in your political climate.

In a way, ScrOG is the opposite in approach to SOG. ScrOG effectively utilizes the available light on just a few plants. The plants are trained to blanket a given area, but these few plants take longer to grow vegetatively. On the other hand, SOG utilizes the available light on the maximum number of plants that can fit into the grow space. The plants are grown vegetatively for only a short amount of time and then flowered to keep their size small and decrease the time until harvest.

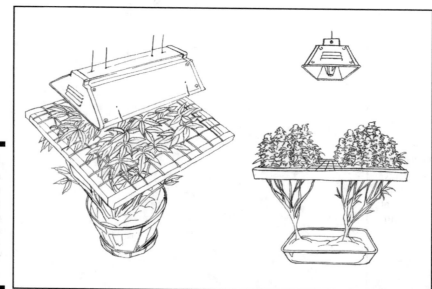

Figure 3-4:
You can bend young stems along the length of a screen to maximize your lighting.

Using Advanced Techniques

You may want consider using either of these techniques depending on your goals and growing situation. However, if you're just starting out, you may want to slowly work your way up to using them. SOG requires good understanding and good practice of developing mother plants and creating a lot of clones. ScrOG requires a fundamental understanding of how a plant grows vegetatively, so that you can effectively train them to grow sideways as they reach the screen.

This book doesn't attempt to fully cover either technique, as they are advanced in nature. If you've already grown a crop or two indoors, you can easily adapt one of these techniques. They are fairly easy to implement if you've already been growing and there is a wealth of information available on the internet that covers the finer details.

Security Issues

Security should always be a top priority when selecting your grow room. Your freedom could come to depend on selecting a stealth grow room with a minimal chance of being "discovered" by nosy neighbors, law enforcement, or kids trying to cure their sobriety. The Grow Room Security chapter is devoted to many aspects of indoor cannabis growing that could compromise your security. This section deals with choosing a grow space that will offer the highest amount of possible security.

There is no such thing as a 100% secure grow room, but you can stack the odds in your favor by considering all the possible ways a grow room can be discovered and exposed. Consider each of the following security aspects and make sure that the room you want to use isn't unnecessarily risky.

> ✺ **Can the grow room be seen from another room or window?**
> This one is a no-brainer; you don't want anyone to see your garden or you tending to your garden. Large or walk-in closets are fairly secure, but you should always close blinds and doors if you plan to be working on your garden.

ꙮ **Is there a place to store your growing tools, nutrient solution, and other items out of sight, yet near the room?**
You don't want to be seen hauling obvious growing supplies to and from your grow space. Keep all of your supplies nearby in a rubber tote box or on nearby shelves. The supplies you use should be as secure as the room you use them in.

ꙮ **Will light leaks from your grow room be a problem when guests visit?**
While the room's contents may be out of sight, powerful HID light can still creep through the edges of the door, under the door, or out of the exhaust/intake vents. While this may be unavoidable, you should try to find a room that's away from unfriendly foot traffic.

ꙮ **Will neighbors notice noise or odor coming from your grow room?**
Only you can gauge the risk your living quarters present to your grow room. The proximity of neighbors and their relative nosiness are two of the larger issues involved in growing marijuana in urban or apartment living. Make sure your walls, ceiling, and floor are thick enough to safely run the necessary equipment without waking the night-shift security guard living upstairs or the 90 year-old great grandmother living below you. Make sure odor is dealt with responsibly by using one of the odor removal techniques found in the Grow Room Security chapter.

ꙮ **Is the room below you another apartment that might get wet from a leaky hydroponic system?**
If you find yourself in this situation, you simply must be more careful and provide more protection in the way of drop cloths, traps, or even placing the main reservoir in a larger, empty reservoir like a plastic kiddie pool. One unnoticed crack or leak could end your growing operation, get your evicted, and get the cops called.

ꙮ **Can you safely exhaust and intake air from outdoors without raising suspicion?**
Apartments, condos, and closely spaced houses can present a problem when your grow room is near exterior walls and windows. You don't always have to draw or expel your air directly outdoors, but it *is* recommended. If you need to vent into one or more rooms to avoid detection, do it.

🌿 **Can you lock the room to keep people from snooping?**
If possible, add a lock to your room, closet, or shed. A nosy friend who *thinks* he smells something can easily confirm it if all he needs to do is open a closet door to find out. A ten-dollar lock or a visit from the police, it should be an easy choice to make.

🌿 **Will heat from the grow lights be noticeable outside the room?**
If the grow room is near a common living area, plan to exhaust odor and hot air away from it. This could be as easy as venting to the attic or as complicated as adding ducting to a previously unconnected room. You don't want friends or family asking you why it's always so hot in your house.

Choosing the Right Spot

Before you decide where you will set up your grow room, ask yourself the following questions to make sure you're picking the best grow space available to you:

✓ **Have I got access to several electrical sockets?**

✓ **Can I get water to the grow room easily?**

✓ **Can I provide fresh air to the room and remove stale air?**

✓ **Will anyone be able to see light spillage?**

✓ **Will anyone be able to hear the ventilation fans?**

✓ **Will anyone be able to smell the plants?**

Remember, putting all of this information into perspective is not easy. It helps to visualize how the growing equipment will fit into the space and how you will interact with it on a daily basis. The following section briefly describes the equipment you need to grow indoors. As you read through the list, try to visually "place" each component into the space you're considering.

Planning Your Grow Room

Make sure you think of the grow room as the living space for your plants. Your harvest depends, to some extent, on the size of area you have to work with. Regardless of how much or how little space you have to devote to the grow room, you must provide vertical (up and down) space for each of the following components:

🌿 **Reservoir tank** (1)
The reservoir tank holds the water and solution that supplies nutrients to your plants. There's no set rule on how large of a reservoir you need for a given number of plants. Generally you want a tank that will supply your plants with one to two weeks worth of nutrients and still remain about half full. The average height of most store-bought reservoirs is one foot.

🌿 **Roots and growing medium** (2)
The plant roots rest in a growing medium that helps them absorb water and nutrients and gives them access to air. Again, there are no set rules on the amount of growing medium or container size. There's no average size, as they can be as shallow as few inches, like a Rockwool slab, or over a foot tall, like a large bucket or pot.

🌿 **Plants (3)**
The plants may begin as small as a few inches and can eventually grow as large as ten feet tall. Realistically, you don't want your plants to grow this tall indoors unless you can provide adequate lighting to the tops as well as the entire length of the plant. Plants mature as small as half a foot, but the ideal size for most indoor situations is two to three feet.

🌿 **A cautious distance between the plant and grow lamp** (4)
Lighting for indoor marijuana cultivation is very bright and can get extremely hot. While exhaust fans can remove hot air from the room and air-cooled lamps allow you to send much of the bulb's heat directly out of the room, the HID lamps need to stay 1-2 feet above the tops of the plants to prevent burning.

🌿 **Lamp** (5)
All things considered, the light you use to mimic the sun's rays may be the single biggest factor in the size of your overall harvest. Read the lighting chapter for more details on how to choose the right lights for your size of room. The average HID (High Intensity Discharge) lamp is ½-1 foot tall.

⚜ Room to grow (6)

When you change your plants' lighting cycle from vegetative (18/6) to flowering (12/12), your plants will continue to grow 50% to 200% larger as they flower. When choosing a grow room, you should factor in how tall you will grow your plants in both the vegetative and flowering phases. It's imperative that you choose a grow room that has enough space for both phases or your plants will grow too close to the lamp, causing scorching to the tops of the plants.

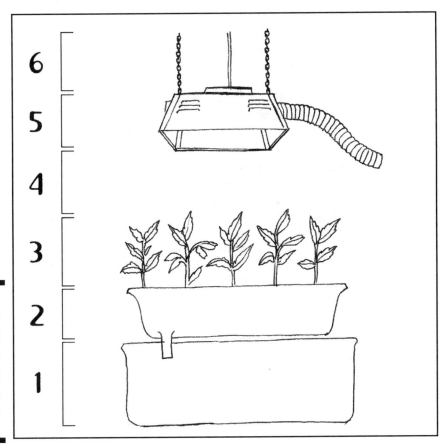

Figure 3-5:
Compare the diagram to your grow room to make sure you have enough vertical space.

You must also provide horizontal (side to side) space for the following:

🌿 **Reservoir and/or growing trays** (1)

If you're going to buy a hydroponics system instead of building one, you need to make sure the grow room is big enough to accommodate the system you want. Fortunately, hydroponics systems come in many shapes and sizes to fit into almost any reasonable space. There isn't an average size for reservoirs and growing trays; just make sure the one you want can fit and has extra room around the sides to work in. Yes, use a tape measure.

🌿 **Water pump** (2)

Some hydroponics systems are built with a water pump in the reservoir tank, so it doesn't take up any additional space. Larger hydroponics systems have their water pump outside of the tank, which takes up more floor space. If you think you will build or buy a system with a water pump outside of the reservoir, plan for it to take up roughly one square foot of floor space.

🌿 **Vents and ducting** (3)

Most popular lighting systems are available with air-cooling flanges as an add-on expense. Air ducting is fastened to the flanges and a venting fan is connected to the other end of the tubing. Air-cooling keeps your grow room cooler by exhausting the heat emitted by the bulb out of the grow room before it escapes the reflector. Ducting can be attached to the wall or suspended from the ceiling. The only rule is to use the least amount of ducting as possible.

🌿 **Ballast** (4)

The ballast serves as the power supply to your grow light, also known as a lamp. Each lamp requires it's own ballast, so the more lamps you use, the more space you need for ballasts. The size of the ballast depends on how powerful (in watts) the lamp is. If your security situation allows, it is good practice to put ballasts outside your grow room because they produce a lot of heat. Ballasts occupy about one square foot, allowing for additional space around the ballast to help dissipate heat. Manufacturers include a long power cord between ballast and lamp so the ballasts can be placed on shelves and out of the way.

⚘ Fans (5)

At least one simple oscillating (back and forth) fan needs to be included in your design. Fans help circulate the air, which helps your plants to breathe. A good rule of thumb is to have one small to medium size fan for every 25 plants you grow. Fans come in all shapes and sizes, but the better fans allow you to attach them to the ceiling or a wall, which saves you additional floor space.

⚘ Exhaust and/or intake fans (6)

Exhaust fans take the hot, stagnant air from the grow room and send it outside the room. Conversely, intake fans bring fresh air from outside the space into the grow room. The appropriate fans for this application can be awkwardly sized, but the best have additional mounting brackets that allow you to place them anywhere inside or outside of your grow room. Plan to mount your fan(s) on a wall or even better, on the ceiling, saving you valuable floor space.

⚘ Power outlets, timers, and meters (7)

While these take up very little space, they should also be part of your design. The main reason you would want to include these is because they need to be placed safely AWAY from the reservoir tank and not on the floor next to it and especially not on top of it near the grow trays and the hoses that supply water to them. Know where your power outlets are and plan accordingly by either building a shelf or even better, a long extension cord that keeps all of this sensitive equipment far away from the waterworks.

⚘ Room to work (8)

You need room to access all of your plants throughout your plants' growth phases. You should be able to reach all of your plants and tend to their needs. This doesn't necessarily require an empty perimeter around the entire hydroponics system as long as you have long arms and a modest number of plants. Your size and flexibility determine how much space you need. Just use common sense and plan for enough empty space to access the entire system and the plants it contains.

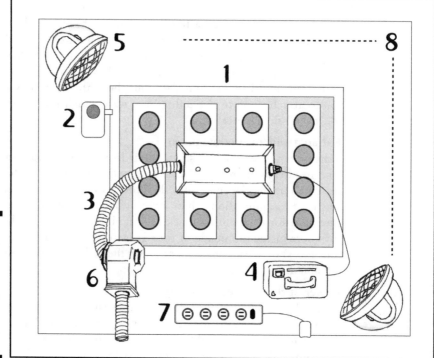

Figure 3-6:
Use the
diagram
to visually
"map" the
location of
all of the
necessary
components.

Creating the Final Plan

Think of your final plan as a tool to help figure out your costs and to ensure that all the components needed to grow your plants — lights, fans, systems, etc. — are eventually purchased and installed.

You can use copies of your plan to start researching the components you need to buy. Surf the internet and visit some of the marijuana web sites that give you the pros and cons of a given piece of equipment. Most equipment manufactures have web sites that let you to view the specifications and prices on virtually everything you need. Most will also give you contact information for the places where you can buy the equipment.

You can also show your plans, without directly referencing what you intend to grow, to the employees of hydroponics stores in your area so they can help you price your setup. If you walk into one of these stores without a plan and without being mindful of your budget, you can find your entire grow room stalled because you don't have everything you need since you've overspent on just the first few components.

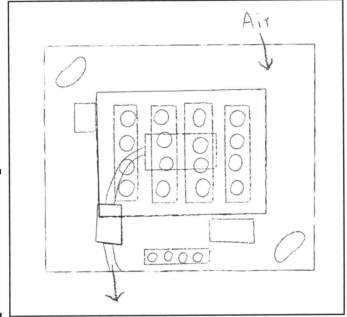

Figure 3-7:
Rough
drawings help
you track
items you
need to buy
and where
they go in
your room.

Follow these steps to create a final plan:

1. **Use a measuring tape to measure the exact dimensions of your grow room.**

    Don't estimate the size, measure it and write it down. Measure the floor space and then the height of the room, multiply those two together and you have the total square footage of your grow room.

2. **Plot each component of the grow room in both floor space and the vertical space.**

    Each component has been described in this chapter, including their average sizes. Draw a square to represent the floor space and draw out the reservoir, the extra working space, and everything else that takes up floor space. Draw the height of the grow room and block out how much space each component will occupy. If you find that you've got extra space, you can use this to grow your plants taller and bushier if you desire.

3. **After you pencil in the components, check your accuracy.**

   When you eyeball the plan and then look at the closet or room, does it seem like everything will fit? Use a measuring tape to visually place where each component will eventually go. You can even use a pencil to mark different lines on the walls that represent the height of the reservoir, plant length, lamp, etc. When it comes time to install your equipment, you will know exactly where everything goes.

4. **Add miscellaneous items.**

   You may want to draw in ducting, shelving for tools, hooks to hang lighting, or anything else that you plan to buy or build. After you've added all of the components and are satisfied that the dimensions are accurate, feel free to ink over the pencil lines and make copies of the design. Obviously, you shouldn't leave your plans laying around for friends and family to ask about.

Keeping Costs Down

At this point, you should have a complete design drawing. You should refer to this as you research and buy your equipment. It's even a good idea to hold on to your plans throughout your first grow to see how closely reality matches your design.

When it comes time to actually make your purchases, consider the following:

- ✓ **Am I buying quality equipment that will last me more than a grow or two?**

- ✓ **Does the shop allow me to return equipment if it doesn't meet my needs? What is their policy?**

- ✓ **Have I researched the equipment and asked others (internet/grow shop/other growers) if it works as advertised?**

- ✓ **Am I overdoing it for my first grow by buying the biggest and best of everything regardless of my actual needs or space limitations?**

Choosing Components

The next part of the book, The Equipment, gives you information on each of the components outlined in your design. As you finalize on the right components for your room, write them down and keep the information with your other planning documents.

When you walk into the hydroponics store, show them your plans, they might even be impressed. Even more important than that is showing them that you have done your research, know what you want, and expect a no-nonsense experience at their shop. If they blow off your plans and try to talk you into buying more or different equipment, walk away. If you want, call the companies of the products you were being talked out of buying and they will point you towards more reputable dealers.

Chapter 4

Lighting

. . . .

In This Chapter

▶ Understanding HID lighting concepts

▶ Getting to know the different types of bulbs

▶ Selecting the right wattage for your space

▶ Maximizing your grow room reflectance

. . . .

Lighting is the single most important factor in an indoor garden and often requires the biggest financial investment. It's important to set up an adequate and cost effective lighting system and to understand the different types of bulbs available, as well as their functions, strengths, and limitations. Of all of the chapters covering equipment, this one is the most important and should not be skipped.

When plants use light energy for growth, they are photosynthesizing. The details of this chemical reaction are complex, but largely irrelevant to the casual or hobby marijuana cultivator. Research into grow lights has been extensive and products are readily available that put this research into use.

Entire books have been written specifically about how plants make use of sunlight, employing a lot of jargon, flow charts and cellular photography. You will find none of that here. What you will find is practical information that distills much of the technical information into just few key decision points and best practice tips.

HID Lamps Explained

New growers can be overwhelmed when trying to choose a HID (High Intensity Discharge) lamp for their grow room. There are many types, strengths and brands available and too much advertising hype for the novice indoor gardener to evaluate and make a good choice. Manufacturers use different and incompatible methods to specify their lamps (initial lumens, mean lumens, PAR, CRI, color temperature, even "radiant flux," among others), making it very difficult to compare these without a degree in physics.

First, let's start with the most basic questions a first-time grower is likely to ask.

What is HID lighting?

HID stands for **High Intensity Discharge**; it is one of the most efficient types of lighting available. The two types of HID lights used for growing plants are Metal Halide (MH) and High Pressure Sodium (HPS). HID lamps are the most intense light source available to the general public; they put out more light than any other grow lamp on the market. HID is also more efficient than other grow lights and can last up to six times longer than the others.

Are HID Lights Safe to Use?

In general, HID lights are very safe. You may not realize it, but HID lighting systems are being used in warehouses, retail and groceries stores, gas stations, sports stadiums, streetlights, and there may even be an HID security/flood light in your back yard. Look for systems that are UL listed to help ensure a safe lighting fixture. UL listing means that the product has been thoroughly tested and certified by the nations top testing labs; they test for proper wire connections, safe components, and proper heat displacement.

What are the differences between MH bulbs and HPS bulbs?

The two main types of high intensity discharge lights available for growing plants are HPS, which stands for High Pressure Sodium and MH, which stands for Metal Halide.

Metal Halide lamps have a balanced light spectrum, which offers the most natural light output and promotes leaf growth. Metal Halide's balanced spectrum contains the common blue and red wavelengths needed by plants for the most rapid growth. Plants can be grown from start to finish using metal halide lighting systems. MH bulbs come in 175, 250, 400, 1000 and 1500-watt sizes.

High Pressure Sodium lamps are more efficient than Metal Halide, producing about 10-15% more lumens per watt than a Metal Halide bulb. HPS emits an orange/yellow color that is similar to the sun's spectrum in the mid-day. This type of light promotes flower growth. However, the lack of blue spectrum light can sometimes make a plant stretch during the vegetative growth phase. HPS grow bulbs comes in 150, 250, 400, 430, 600 and 1000-watt sizes.

Metal Halide lamps work best for vegetative growth and as a primary light source for any plant. High Pressure Sodium lamps work best for fruiting and flowering plants. Low wattage fluorescent tubes works best for seedlings and clones.

How many hours should I keep my lights on in my garden?

The amount of time your garden should be exposed to light depends on what "cycle" or growth phase your garden is in:

The vegetative cycle of your garden starts with the sprouting of your seedlings and can be continued indefinitely. In the vegetative cycle, your garden will require a minimum of 16-18 hours of light and 6-8 hours of darkness daily, although some growers give their plants continuous lighting 24 hours a day to maximize vegetative growth.

The flowering or "budding" cycle is usually equal amounts of light and dark; 12 hours on, 12 hours off, also known as 12/12. This produces a change in the plants metabolism, simulating fall and is the cycle that the plants will show their sex.

Usually, you will be able to determine the sex of a plant within the first two weeks of 12/12. By the third week, most plants have developed healthy bud sites or pollen sacks. The plants will continue on the 12/12 cycle until harvest. The flowering cycle lasts 45-90 days depending on the genetic strain, but the average is about eight weeks for indoor strains.

How much light do I need?

A very general rule of thumb is that your garden needs 30-50 watts of HID lighting per square foot of area (WPSF). This rule ignores the shape of your garden, so the following is really a better guide:

A 250-watt HID will illuminate a 2´x 2´ garden.

A 400-watt HID will illuminate a 3´ x 3´ garden.

A 600-watt HID will illuminate a 3.5´x 3.5´ garden.

A 1000-watt HID will illuminate a 4´x 4´ garden.

These numbers assume you have a good reflector around your bulb and reflective wall coverings. You can increase the figures a bit if using multiple bulbs, due to their overlapping effect. You can also increase coverage using a light mover.

The chart above takes into consideration that WPSF assumes that the bulb's intensity is equal over the entire grow area. In other words each square foot/meter receives the same number of lumens. But in reality, light diminishes rapidly the farther you go from the bulb (¼ the intensity for each doubling of the distance). So each bulb has a limited range, beyond which you do not have good growth.

For example, a grow space that's 2 x 10 feet would require 1000 watts if you go by the 50 WPSF guideline that's commonly mentioned. But a 1000-watt bulb only covers an area about five feet across — meaning the edges of your garden will be dark. A better choice in this case would be three 400 or two 600-watt bulbs.

Another problem with WPSF is that it assumes that all bulbs have the same intensity. But 1000 watts of high intensity light is not the same as 1000 watts of fluorescent or incandescent light. Fluorescent tubes have their lumens spread out over a long tube and are therefore dim. Incandescent lights have the wrong color spectrum and are also dim.

Types of Lighting Systems

There are many different types of bulbs you could use to grow indoors, but there are only a few that you *should* use. For example, ordinary household bulbs, also known as incandescent bulbs, are a terrible source of light for growing plants because they don't emit light in the necessary spectrum.

Other types of everyday bulbs, like halogens and mercury vapor lamps are equally unsuitable. Metal Halide, High Pressure Sodium, and florescent bulbs are the only types of bulbs you should consider for your grow. Read on to find out why.

High Pressure Sodium (HPS)

HPS bulbs are the most efficient bulbs commonly used by hobby gardeners. They are high in the red and yellow parts of the spectrum and low in the blue, which imitates the fall sun. Because of this spectrum, marijuana plants that are grown using only HPS lights can grow elongated and rather stringy. For plants like marijuana that naturally bud and flower in the fall, HPS is usually the light of choice because the light spectrum promotes flower (bud) production.

HPS bulbs range from 35 to 1000 watts, with the 250w, 400w, 600w and 1000w being the most popular for indoor horticulture. HPS bulbs should be replaced after about 24 months. The bulbs slowly lose their brightness over time and to maintain good light quality, the bulbs must be changed before the end of their rated life.

Enhanced Performance HPS

Standard High Pressure Sodium lamps emit an orange/yellow color that is similar to the sun's spectrum in the mid day. This type of light promotes flower growth. However, as mentioned above, the lack of blue spectrum light in Standard HPS bulbs can sometimes make a plant stretch during the vegetative growth phase. Enhanced Performance HPS lamps have a wider blue spectrum, which makes a significant difference in plant growth.

Metal Halide (MH)

Metal halide bulbs are very efficient and produce a light that is close to full summer sun, with a spectrum rich in the blue end. This promotes fast vegetative growth and compact, stocky plants with short internodal leaf spacing.

MH bulbs come in sizes from 70 to 1500 watts with the 250w, 400w and the 1000w being the most popular sizes for gardening. All of the MH bulbs need to be used with a ballast that is designed to run that bulb's specific size. Medal Halide bulbs (except the 1000w Super Bulb) should be replaced about every 18 months (assuming an 18 hour per day "on" cycle). The 1000w super bulbs don't last as long as the others and should be replaced every 12 months.

A grower who uses MH alone for vegetative growth, then switches to HPS on the first day after initiating flowering (their first night), can expect the quickest and most pronounced bud set. This is because the sodium light closely mimics the spectrum of the late fall sun, indicating that fall is approaching. The plant thinks that winter is going to sneak up and kill it, so it freaks out and tries to complete its life cycle before the frost.

Super Horizontal MH

Super Horizontal lamps provide 12% more light output than a standard metal halide, but must be burned in a horizontal position. Metal Halide lamps provide a light that is blue-orientated in the spectrum. It's the best type of light to be used as a primary light source (if little or no natural sunlight is available). This type of light promotes plant growth.

Conversion Bulbs

To spare the expense of two systems, conversion bulbs might be your best option. Conversion bulbs are specially designed to run off one type of ballast but provide the other spectrum of light. This allows the gardener to operate one light system and switch bulbs according to the phase of growth (vegetative or flowering).

HPS conversion bulbs run on an MH ballast and emit more lumens and red spectrum light than an MH bulb in the same ballast. You can start plants under MH lamps and then switch to an HPS conversion bulb for flowering.

MH conversion bulbs offer the opposite approach. You start with an MH conversion bulb in an HPS lighting system and then switch to a regular HPS bulb for flowering.

Conversion bulbs are most commonly used to convert a MH lighting system into one that can provide HPS light. This is an inexpensive alternative to buying another complete lighting system to obtain the benefits of HPS light. Although conversion bulbs are more expensive than traditional HID bulbs, they can give you more initial flexibility, allowing you to provide your plants with two types of light from a single lighting system.

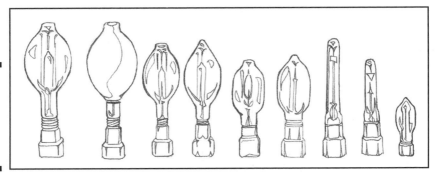

Figure 4-1:
HID bulbs come in a variety of shapes and sizes.

Only using an HPS or MH Lamp

Using only one type of bulb throughout a plant's life cycle or switching bulbs when changing growth phases affects only yield, not potency or time until harvest/maturation. The buds produced using a single bulb-type will not be as dense as those that use both. Gardens that rely solely on HPS lighting with no MH lighting during the vegetative phase will show a more pronounced effect such as stringy plants.

The light spectrum cast by HPS lights — although wonderful for inducing flowering — consists mostly of orange-red tints. These tints induce more stretching between the internodes during vegetative growth. Internodal spacing is the most direct correlation between growth characteristics and yield. Metal halide lights are meant to mimic summer daylight and using these lights alone during the vegetative cycle, along with keeping lights as close as you can without burning them, will help you get the tightest internodal spacing.

Lighting Systems Components

This section provides a brief description for all of the components of an HID lamp. Subsequent sections provide in-depth information on the various types of each component to help you which system(s) you need for your grow room.

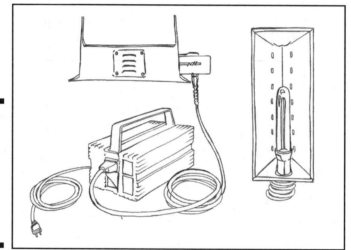

Figure 4-2:
A complete
lighting
system
includes
bulb, ballast,
reflector,
hood, and
power cords.

⚘ Bulb

Each type of horticulture bulb works in a different way, but they are all designed to provide plants with intense light in the correct color spectrum to replace the light they normally receive from the sun. Different types of bulbs can be used during different growth phases to give plants the correct color spectrum for that particular phase. Choosing the right wattage and type of bulb is one of the most important factors you must consider when buying equipment for your grow room.

⚘ Reflector

A reflector is attached above the bulb and helps redirect light back down towards the garden. A quality reflector provides superb light distribution and uniformity of light over the crop. Reflectors can increase available light by up to thirty percent and can double or even triple the total growing area. Reflectors are usually included with the light fixture.

⚜Vents/Ducting

Most popular lighting systems are available with air-cooling flanges as an add-on feature. Air ducting is fastened to the flanges and a venting fan is connected to the other end of the tubing. Air-cooling keeps your grow room cooler by exhausting the heat emitted by the bulb out of the grow room before it escapes the reflector.

⚜Hood

The hood is the enclosure that houses the bulb, the reflector, and in some cases, the ballast itself. Most hoods come in the same general shape, but vary in size depending on reflector and bulb size. The only thing you need to consider regarding hoods is whether you will want to connect it to ducting so you can air-cool the bulb.

⚜Protective Glass

The glass face below the bulb protects the plants and the bulb from each other. Bulbs should never be touched by anything while in operation and should be wiped clean if they are ever touched. Glass prevents water or mist from accidentally touching the bulb, which would most likely cause it to crack or worse. Additionally, if you plan to air cool the lamp, the glass encloses the bulb, allowing you to remove most of the heated air it produces before it can reach your plants.

Bulbs and Ballasts

In lighting systems, a ballast provides the proper voltage to establish an arc between two electrodes, regulates the electric current flowing through the lamp to stabilize light output, and ultimately supplies the correct voltage required for proper lamp operation and compensates for voltage variations in the electrical current.

HID bulbs generally need specific ballasts and any given ballast can usually safely and effectively operate only one type or a few types of HID bulbs.

WEED WARNING

The bulb wattage must be matched to the ballast. A smaller bulb will usually be fed a wattage close to what the proper bulb takes and will generally overheat and may catastrophically fail. Any catastrophic failures may not necessarily happen quickly. A larger bulb will be underpowered and will operate at reduced efficiency and may have a shortened lifespan. The ballast may also overheat from prolonged operation with an oversized bulb that fails to warm.

Even if the ballast and bulb wattages match, you shouldn't use a MH bulb with an HPS system or vice-versa. Many HPS lamps require a high voltage starting pulse provided only by ballasts made to power such lamps.

Switchable ballasts

Switchable ballasts allow you to run both metal halide and high pressure sodium bulbs from a single ballast; you just insert the appropriate bulb and set the switch to the correct operating setting. This type of ballast enables growers to bypass costly conversion lamps and maintain the higher light output from non-conversion bulbs.

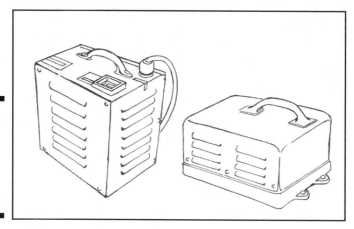

Figure 4-3:
Ballast size is determined largely by its wattage capacity.

Bulb replacement

Unlike the lamps in your home, HID lamps should be replaced before they burn out. HPS lamps should be replaced at least every two years. MH should be replaced at least once every year. Although these lamps may look like they are fine and could likely light up for up to six years, you will not get the most out of your lamp.

After one year (12-14 hours a day) of use, your MH lamp will put out around 65% to 70% of the initial lumen output. For example, your 1000w MH lamp puts out 110,000 lumens, so after one year of use it puts out around 71,500 lumens. You are still using 1000 watts of power to generate 65% of the light. The life of HPS lamps is greater; after one year most HPS lamps give about 85 to 90% of the initial light output.

If your wallet can take the hit, buy an extra bulb and keep it handy for when your original bulb begins to dim or when an accidental bump or other mishap sends your cracked bulb to the garbage can.

Reflectors

After the bulb itself, the reflector is the most important part of a grow light. The reflector is the deciding factor in how much light will be reflected on the plants and how uniform the light is. You want to have an even distribution of light over the entire growing area.

Reflectors accomplish this by reflecting light being emitted away from the plants back toward the plants. Manufacturers use computer aided design and highly reflective materials to create an assortment of reflector-types. The two main categories of reflector-types are horizontal and vertical.

Horizontal reflectors

Horizontal reflectors are by far the most common reflector used for plant lighting. They do an excellent job concentrating the light in a downward direction (where the plants are), giving your plants more intense coverage. The only disadvantage to horizontal hoods is the amount of heat that is directed downward. You can overcome the heat problem with fans and blowers as long the reflector can be air-cooled.

Sound lighting depends strongly on how efficiently the light is distributed. Horizontal reflectors are the most efficient reflectors as well as the most popular. A horizontal lamp position increases light up to 40% over a lamp burning in the vertical position.

Vertical reflectors

Vertical reflectors look like a large umbrella and do a good job spreading light in a large area. They also have more room for heat to dissipate so you can place them closer to your plants. The disadvantages of the vertical hoods are that they throw light everywhere and you have plenty of wasted light. In short, vertical reflectors are not recommended for small grow rooms.

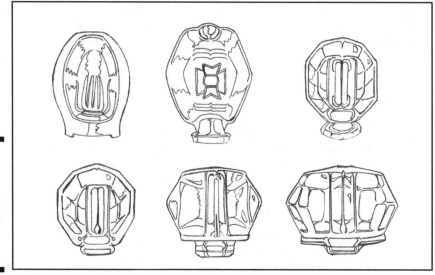

Figure 4-4:
Reflector
size and
shape
determine
how light is
distributed to
your plants.

Hoods

If you've selected your bulb-type and wattage, the hard part is over with. Now you need to decide if your grow room will get hot enough to require air cooling or if you think you would like to use a dual-bulb fixture. The following section explains your options.

Air cooled

Some fixtures come with hoods designed to contain the bulb and ventilate the fixture itself. The bulb is sealed into the hood with a piece of high temperature glass. The hood has a 3 or 4-inch hole on both sides, which are used to connect it to a vent hose. An exhaust fan is attached to one end and fresh air is constantly circulated around the bulb, venting the heat out of the garden.

Dual fixture

A two-in-one fixture is the best of both worlds, providing a spectrum that is as close to ideal as possible with artificial lighting. Dual fixtures provide sockets and ballasts for both MH and HPS bulbs to run inside the same fixture. Both bulbs are run at the same time throughout the entire life cycle of your plants, giving your plants the best lighting possible. Dual fixtures are certainly not necessary for a successful garden and consideration must be made to the heat that is produced from a single fixture containing two high-wattage bulbs.

Figure 4-5: The hood determines which reflectors can be used.

HID Lighting Safety

There's always a certain amount of risk involved when using HID lamps. Shattering the bulb is the most serious danger. You must be extremely careful not to get the bulb wet in any way. If you mist your plants, move the light up first and be very careful not to overspray and hit the lamp. Even the moisture from your hands can cause it to break under the right conditions; wear gloves when you handle them.

Replace your bulbs regularly (every 12 to 24 months depending bulb type and on usage) and buy good quality fixtures. But don't be too concerned, millions of people work around these lights every day with few serious side effects.

Fluorescent Lighting

A fluorescent light is made up of a glass tube coated with phosphor, which is filled with a mixture of gases. When electrical current is applied, it "excites" the gases, causing the tube to glow brightly. Fluorescent tubing is coated with phosphor, which determines the color of the bulb.

Fluorescent tubes are available in many shapes and sizes, but the most widely used diameter tube size is between .25 and 1.5 inches. There are a large variety of tube lengths as well, from 6 to 96 inch, but the most widely used is a 48-inch fixture. Fluorescent lights are available from 4 to 214 watts, with the most popular being 40-watt dual bulb fixtures.

Fluorescent tubes do get warm, but not if they have adequate air circulation. A simple fan blowing over the fixtures will help a great deal to cool the tubes. If it's done properly, any stray foliage that comes in contact with the tubes will not be harmed.

Fluorescent Bulb Color Spectrums

One way light is measured is on a **Kelvin** scale. A Kelvin scale expresses the exact color the bulb emits. Bulbs in the range of 2700 to 6500 on a Kelvin scale are ideal for growing marijuana. Plants respond not only to the quantity of light, but also the quality.

Fluorescent bulbs have the widest spectrum range than any other bulb. The tubes come in various spectrums, determined by the type of phosphor the bulb is coated with. The following fluorescent types are as listed, along with what they may accomplish for you.

Full spectrum
This type of bulb of bulb has all the colors of the Kelvin scale. This bulb is good for vegetation phase. Note: This spectrum fluorescent is used in hospitals nationwide in helping people with "depression".

Wide spectrum
These bulbs will restrict development of side branching, helps plants mature faster. This fluorescent is high in the red, orange and yellow color range. In fact, this fluorescent is much like an HPS color range, which makes it the best all around choice for the flowering phase.

Daylight spectrum
These types of bulbs are very high (if not the highest) in the blue range on the Kelvin scale. This fluorescent promotes an arctic blue look. This fluorescent bulb is recommended during the vegetative phase.

☙ **Cool spectrum**

This bulb-type will promote multiple side growth, nice green foliage. This fluorescent is high in the blue range, giving off a bright white appearance. This fluorescent bulb is recommended for the vegetative phase.

☙ **Warm spectrum**

This fluorescent will promote extra thick stems and branches, and will give you about 5% denser buds than other spectrums. This fluorescent is high in the red range on the Kelvin scale. This fluorescent is recommended for the flowering phase.

Reflective Wall Covering

An easy way to help maximize your lighting investment is by choosing an efficient wall covering for your grow room. Your walls should reflect as much of the light that escapes from the lamp (spillage) and reflect it back onto the plants. Light that never gets to your plants is wasted in terms of growth and electricity. Since both your plant's health and bud density are directly related to the amount of light they get, it only makes sense to provide as much light as possible to your garden.

To get the best results with your light and walls, it's important to get the walls as close as possible to your garden to ensure that the least amount of light is wasted. Some growers attach their reflective material to false walls so they can move them closer and then further away as the plants grow, always keeping them within inches of their plants.

Reflectance

A **reflectance rating** tells you how much light is reflected by a surface. The high percentage presents the best possible circumstances for that material (for example a 99% reflectivity rating for Mylar sheeting would be under ideal conditions: no creases, completely flat, no discoloration, etc.).

The following table lists some construction materials and paint colors and their reflectance ratings:

Table 4-1		Reflectance Ratings	
Material	**Reflectance**	**Color**	**Reflectance**
Mirror	95%	White	70-80%
Polished metal	85-95%	Light green	45-50%
Mylar	92%	Red	20-25%
White poly	70-85%	Dark green	10-15%
Plaster	80%	Black	0-5%
White glazed tiles	60-75%		
Aluminum foil	60-70%		
Concrete	15-40%		
Clear glass	6-8%		

Below are details on some of the materials listed in the reflectance chart, including their advantages and disadvantages:

Flat white paint

High-temperature white spray paint is a good choice as a durable, reflective finish. It's nearly as reflective as "specular" aluminum inserts seen in HID hoods. A can of high-temperature white paint costs less than most other reflective options and is easily obtained at hardware and auto part stores. If they offer a choice between flat white and glossy, choose the flat white. Spray five or six light coats on the walls or substitute walls (plywood, drywall, or anything flat and sturdy) until one side looks pure white.

Mylar

Mylar resembles a sturdier version of aluminum foil, but is actually made of plastic. Mylar is considered is one of the best reflective surfaces, reflecting about 98% of all light.

Mylar sheets can be rather hard to work with and a slight breeze will cause it to flap around unless you tack or staple it into place. Mylar comes in three different roll lengths and two different thicknesses, 1 mil. and 2 mil. (a mil. is 1/1000th of an inch) The 2 mil. is strongly recommended because it's easier to work with and has more strength and durability.

Black and white poly

Black and white poly sheeting is very tough and its white side reflects 90% of all light. It can be handled on a daily basis without damage or tearing. And because it's made of plastic, it can be used to partition off spaces to ensure maximum efficiency of your lighting.

Aluminum foil

If aluminum foil is all that is available to you, it can be used as a reflective material, but you should use the dull side to reflect light as the shinny side produces concentrated hot spots. When aluminum foil gets crinkled, its reflective ability is diminished and actually wastes light by causing it to bounce in undesired directions. Using aluminum foil can be a cheap alternative to using Mylar or white paint, but it doesn't perform nearly as well and isn't recommended.

Mirrors

Mirrors are perfect reflectors and don't absorb light as is commonly purported, but are not recommend because of their property of specular reflectivity. Conventional mirrors do not scatter the light onto the garden, they only concentrate it where you don't want it, creating hot spots on your plants, which causes them to burn and wither.

Cleaning Your Wall Covering

Over time, your Mylar will become spotted and stained, especially if you do a lot of foliar feeding!

1. Use a squirt bottle to thoroughly spray down the surface area of the dirty Mylar using soapy water.
2. Clean the Mylar in a downward motion with the wet sponge in a downward stroking pattern. (This will push what dirt the sponge doesn't pick up to the bottom of your sheet for easy removal.)
3. Now that the dirt has been removed, liberally spray the surface of the Mylar with standard glass cleaner.
4. Using the same downward pattern, wipe the Mylar clean with paper towels.

Seedling Lighting

Once seedlings have sprouted, they are ready to begin photosynthesis; which means they will need some light. The seedlings can be placed under metal halide or fluorescent light. The lights are left on for 18 to 24 hours a day.

Many gardeners like to start their seedlings under standard 40-watt fluorescent tube lighting. These lights may be placed about two inches from the tops of the seedlings. As the seedlings grow, keep the tubes close to the top of the seedlings. If more than one of these fluorescent lights is being used, then they are placed parallel to each other, about six inches apart.

WEED WARNING

Fluorescent lighting is generally a poor light source for flowering and budding because of their low output, so you will want to switch the type of light you provide when you plants reach about a foot tall.

Metal halide lights can be used with seedlings, but they are powerful and you must be careful when using them with seedlings. A stationary 250-400 watt light should be placed about three feet above the tops of the seedlings. The seedlings should be monitored every few minutes for the first few hours for burn damage. The light may be lowered six inches a day until the light is about two feet above the top of the seedlings. Seedlings should be carefully monitored each time you lower the light. Any indication of burning means you should immediately raise the lights to their previous height.

Get ready!

The best nutrients are specifically calibrated
for each phase of plant growth.

The type and intensity of bulb used is one of the most
important aspects in determining your yield.

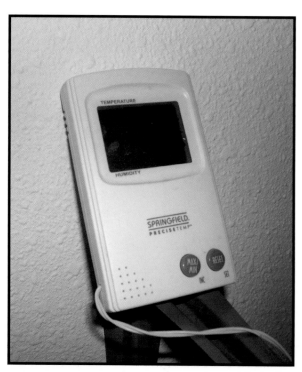

A thermometer is an essential part of any grow room.

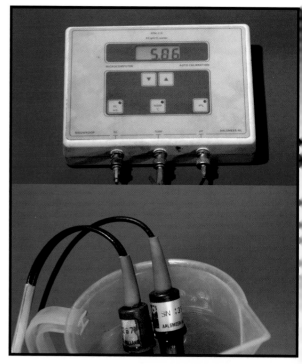

Nutrients are measured in parts per million.
Meters must be calibrated before using.

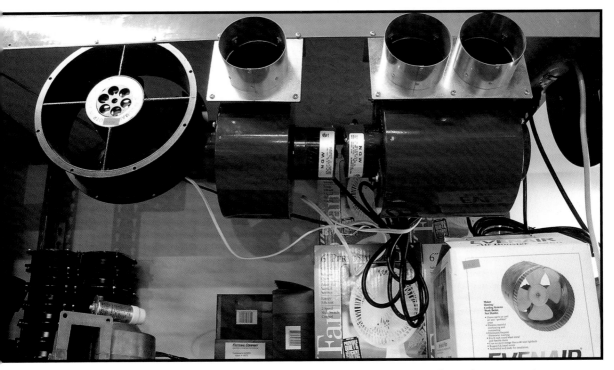

Industrial strength fans are used to both drive fresh air into a room and expel stagnant air. High-quality fans are rated by the amount of cubic air they can exchange per minute.

High intensity discharge lamps utilize hoods and reflectors to maximize light intensity towards the growing area. Each hood is designed to illuminate a specific grow room "footprint".

Mylar sheeting should be tacked or stapled to the grow room walls to maximize lighting efficiency.

An attic can make an ideal grow room as long as temperature and ventilation are a top priority.

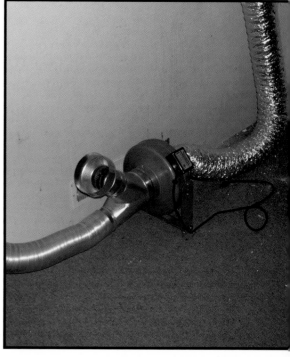

Ducting can be attached to hoods to remove heat before it reaches the plants.

Fresh air should be driven from near the floor and stagnant air should be expelled near the ceiling.

All other elements being equal, the strains you choose to grow determine the quality of your bud.

The moist paper towel method is one of the most effective ways to germinate your seeds.

Germinated seeds should be transplanted to rooting cubes as they grow into seedlings.

Place rooting cubes under florescent lighting while they establish roots before using HID lighting.

Seedlings need much more supervision than plants in the vegetative phase. Always test seedlings under HID lighting for five to ten minutes before leaving them.

Cuttings can be used to "sex" a plant, but they should be labeled to track which plants turn male or female.

The humidity created inside of a dome helps the plants stand upright until they establish roots.

This seedling hasn't grown enough roots to be transplanted to the main grow room.

This seedling has established an extensive rooting system and is ready to be transplanted.

Clones, like seedlings, need to establish enough roots to support themselves.

Once a set of clones have been transplanted, you can begin taking a new set from your mother plants.

Preflowers generally appear after the fourth week of vegetative growth.

Male preflowers appear as small balls, but their most recognizable feature is their lack of pistils.

With most strains of Cannabis, the sex of the plant is identifiable by the second week of flowering.

By the middle of the flowering phase, the flowers on the male plants begin to bloom and release pollen.

On a female plant, a single flower is called a pistil and each grows two small hairs called stigmas.

Female preflowers do not show pistils until after the preflowers have emerged.

If pollen from male plants enter the stigmas, the female becomes fertilized and seed production begins.

Females produce resin on leaves and flowers to protect their seeds even if they have not been pollinated.

By removing the primary growing shoot or "top", the plant redirects its energy to the next two closest shoots.

The two remaining shoots become new primary shoots. Removing these shoots will create four primary shoots.

To create a "sea of green," the vegetative plants in this system will be topped two times to create four primary shoots per plant which develop into an even canopy of tops.

When tying down a plant, gently tie the string to the stem, taking care not to break or crush it.

Find or make holes near the base of your plants to tie the other end of the string to.

By tying down your plants you increase the amount of light intensity to the middle and lower nodes, helping them develop larger, more resinous buds.

If you wait too long to tie down or stake your plants, it can be extremely difficult to manage their growth.

Large colas sag to the ground if they aren't supported by stakes.

By tying your plants to stakes at an angle, you increase the amount of light to the length of your plants as well as help support their weight.

Large grow rooms can involve hundreds of plants, dozens of lights, and extensive ducting.

Some grow rooms might not involve not much more than a corner, a light, and single plant.

Industrial-sized grow rooms require the efforts of many people and the risks involved can be tremendous. The laws in your area should be consulted before building large grow rooms.

Two weeks after the flowering phase began.

Four weeks.

Six weeks.

Leaves should be kept clean of dust and inspected for signs of infestation or nutrient lockout.

Plants use leaves as solar collectors, so they should be positioned to receive maximum exposure to the light.

As the plants mature and flower, the large fan leaves naturally begin to wilt and drop off the plant. Leaves near the bud sites protect the buds and should generally be left alone.

One well-trained plant after three weeks of flowering.

Another single plant after six weeks of flowering.

By extensive use of tying down, staking, and topping techniques, a single female can be trained to mature into a bushy, high-yielding plant.

Chapter 5

Fans

· ·

In This Chapter

▶ Learning how fans help plants grow

▶ Designing your grow room airflow

▶ Selecting the right fans and ducting

▶ Maintaining your grow room temperature and humidity

· ·

Plants use CO_2 (Carbon Dioxide) found in the atmosphere to aid their growth through the processes of photosynthesis and respiration. Plants require the carbon element found in CO_2 and release the leftover oxygen back into the air to the benefit of many other creatures. In an outdoor environment, with even a slight breeze, plants have plenty of available CO_2 to sustain and encourage growth.

Since you will be growing your plants indoors, fans will play a crucial role in providing your grow room with a constant supply of fresh air. Without the use of fans to bring fresh air into your grow room and fans to circulate that air, your plants will use all of the CO_2 next to the leaf surface. When this air is used and no fresh air is forced into its place, dead air space forms that stifles the stomata, slows growth, and creates an environment that encourages disease and pest problems.

The following chapter explains how to design the air flow through your grow room in order to provide your plants with optimal amounts of CO_2. You will also learn how proper airflow helps remove heat produced by HID lighting to keep temperature and humidity in the appropriate range.

Why Airflow is Important?

Besides all of the side benefits of providing fresh air to your plants, the main purpose is to keep your plants "breathing," which encourages photosynthesis and plant growth. Just like nutrients and light, CO_2 is a major building block for growth. Plants access the CO_2 in the atmosphere through their leaves and more specifically, the leaves' stomata.

Stomata are microscopic pores that are located on the undersides of the leaves. Stomata regulate the flow of gasses into and from the plant. Because they can get clogged with dust, filmy residues, pollen, etc., it is very important to have air movement to keep these pores clean and free.

Good air flow design also helps lower grow room temperature by exchanging air heated by grow lamps with cooler air from outside the room. Good airflow also maintains moderate humidity to keep the grow area dry. Keeping humidity in check can help reduce mold on flowers and walls and retard algae on growing mediums.

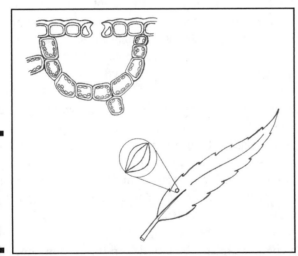

Figure 5-1:
Microscopic stomata enable plants to transpire oxygen as waste.

Planning Air Movement

In general, air movement should be in a straight line: from the intake source, through the plants, toward the exhaust fan and out of the garden. Directional air movement helps keep temperatures and humidity levels constant, supplies CO_2 to the crops, and keeps down bug and disease problems.

Before you start buying any fans or knocking out holes in your walls, you need to familiarize yourself with how to get fresh air into your room, how to circulate that air, and how to remove it when it's no longer beneficial to your plants. The following three sections, Air Intake Source, Oscillating Fans, and Exhaust Venting explain the basics of how air should flow through your room and what equipment you can use to do it.

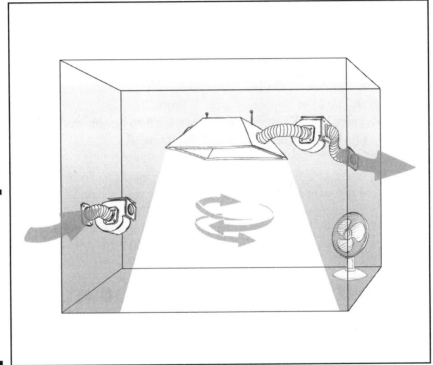

Figure 5-2: Arrows indicate air movement into the room where it circulates, then gets expelled by an exhaust fan.

Air intake source

Fresh air from outside the grow room is an important source of CO_2 when gardens are grown without CO_2 enrichment. You should first consider your room's air intake source. This can be a simple as a hole in the wall or an air intake fan connected via ducting.

Your air intake source is used to bring fresh air containing carbon dioxide to your plants for growth processes. The air intake source also helps maintain the proper garden temperature by replacing the hot air produced by your grow lamp with mild (70-75°F) temperature air from outside the room.

Oscillating fans

Oscillating fans are essential components of a grow room because they help to circulate air from the intake source throughout the room, making CO_2 available to all of your plants. Oscillating fans also help maintain the correct garden temperature throughout the grow space by sending fresh, mild temperature air throughout the room. Additionally, oscillating fans discourage pest and disease problems and encourage stronger stem development due to the gentle sway of the circulated air.

Exhaust fan and ducting

Despite being the last "movement" of your airflow, exhaust vents and fans are the most important aspect to providing an optimal atmosphere for your plants. Without a way for stale air to be removed, there is no point in providing fresh air or circulating it around.

Using an exhaust fan helps remove hot, moist air from your garden, making way for fresh, CO_2-rich air provided by your air intake source. Removing this stagnant air also helps to maintain the correct garden temperature and humidity levels and discourages disease and pest problems.

Creating an Air Intake Source

Stale air that is expelled from the room using an exhaust fan will need to be replaced by fresh air. Fresh air can be brought in by one of three methods. By creating a simple hole or vent in the opposite wall, adding an intake fan that actively draws fresh air from directly outside the room, or using an intake fan attached to ducting that actively draws air from a distant room or completely outside your dwelling. These three options are given further consideration below and are listed in their ease of implementation.

Regardless of the sophistication of your air intake source, the location should be at one end of garden, usually at the opposite end from the exhaust fan system, near the floor. Also remember that cold intake air can harm crops and hot air can't cool the garden, so your situation may require ducting to another room not directly connected to the grow room.

WEED WARNING

The intake source can be a possible entry source for pests and disease, especially if fresh air is brought in from the outdoors. Hang No-Pest strips near the entrance of the intake source to discourage "home invasions" by pests.

Vents

When ventilating any space, the volume of air that gets sucked out of the room also has to be replaced with fresh air. You can't expect to ventilate a grow space by simply sucking air out and not providing an intake vent to replenish what you have removed. You can easily accomplish this by adding a passive intake vent to your grow room.

A passive intake is a purposely made hole, normally located at the bottom of a grow room, centrally opposite an exhaust blower, that provides a gateway for cool air to enter. The term passive means that it is an inactive part of your air flow design. If you plan to operate a closet-sized grow room, an intake vent or two is probably all you will need as long as an exhaust fan is in place.

Will my plants get enough fresh air through a few small holes?
If you use an air exhaust fan without air intake vents, a vacuum is created in your grow room because air is being sucked out and there are no open vents to alleviate the pressure created. This is why one or more air intake vents are required. As stale air is sucked out, cool air is drawn in through the open vent by the suction or vacuum created in the grow room.

Creating an air intake vent

The vent you create should be slightly larger than the exhaust. Using a bigger intake vent or multiple vents allows the air to be drawn in at a lower velocity (speed), which minimizes mixing up of the air in the area and allows the fan to operate more efficiently.

Intake Fans

Most hobby marijuana growers don't use a fan to blow air into their grow rooms. The main reason for this is because one exhaust fan can expel stale air and draw in enough fresh air to keep plants healthy if the room is small or moderate-sized. It's also just an added cost and complication that isn't necessary for small-scale gardening.

Having said that, you may have a rather large closet or an entire room devoted to your "hobby" and even a large exhaust fan is insufficient to keep the grow room supplied with fresh air. You may also want to draw your fresh air from a source located away from the grow room like a chimney, the basement, or outside.

The major difference between an intake fan and an exhaust fan is that instead of sucking air out, you are blowing air in. You also have much less to worry about concerning where expelled air (read: pungent and hot) ends up.

You can choose to run your intake fan 24 hours a day, only when the lights are on, or connected to a sophisticated timer that activates when temperature or CO_2 content reaches inappropriate levels. If you don't have the means or access to such a timer, it is recommended that you run your intake fan while your lights are on.

If you plan to use an intake fan, you should still add one or more intake vents to the room. This is done to avoid any pressure-related problems caused by two competing fans and will reduce stress on both of them. If you do plan to use an intake fan, you should still add one or more intake vents to the room. This is done to avoid any pressure-related problems caused by two competing fans and will reduce stress on both of them.

Ducting

Ducting is only recommended if it is also attached to an air intake fan. Although you may be tempted to attach ducting to your intake "hole," you should avoid it because it will place an incredible amount of strain on your exhaust fan and shorten its lifespan.

Ducting is recommended if you are using an air intake fan and you want to draw your fresh air from another room or from outside your home. Other than deciding where exactly you want to get your fresh air from, the considerations you must make for intake ducting are almost identical to exhaust ducting.

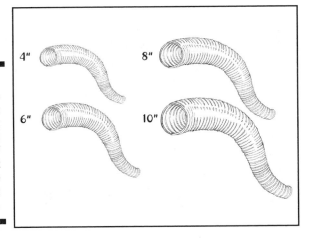

Figure 5-3:
Ducting is
available in
many sizes;
check you
fans intake/
exhaust
ports for the
size you
need.

Oscillating Fans

Oscillating fans are the most effective devices for circulating air in a room. The gentle back and forth sway of the fan is very beneficial for developing plants. These fans tend to keep anaerobic molds down by constantly freshening any potentially stagnant air. Home improvement stores carry a large array of air-moving fans. There are wall-mounted styles available and most are relatively inexpensive.

As well as providing excellent air exchange and keeping air fresh, the breeze from circulating fans can help keep the temperature down, especially from high intensity discharge (HID) grow lights.

Circulation Strengthens Plants

The importance of internal air circulation inside your grow room cannot be stressed enough. A slight breeze will exercise your plants and make them grow stronger, while reducing many hazards that could ruin your crop. Strengthening stalks and stems is vital, as a marijuana plant must prepare itself to withstand the added weight of its blossoming floral clusters (buds). Without strong stalks, the plant might topple over near the end of the plant's flowing phase.

Your oscillating fan(s) should be placed near your crops and close to the intake air source or vent. If the fan can be mounted on the walls, it should be mounted level with the height of the plants. Position the fans to move air evenly through the crop and towards the exhaust fan. If you are transplanting small plants into the space, raise the fans to blow air above these plants until root systems are further established and stems have thickened.

Some growers use oscillating fans 24 hours a day regardless of the lighting cycle. Others use their fans only when the lights are on to save electricity and to minimize noise. At a minimum, circulating fans should be turned on when intake and exhaust fans are running, but it is recommended that your circulation fans stay on 24 hours a day.

Figure 5-4:
For most rooms, an oscillating fan works best, but there are many options.

Exhaust Fan and Ducting System

There are a couple of considerations to make when planning your ventilation. They're pretty simple concepts, but often overlooked.

First, remember that warm air naturally rises to the top of any room and that cool air naturally settles towards the bottom. Since the objective is to remove as much warm air as possible and replace it with cooler air, it's most efficient to place the exhaust as close to the top of the space as possible and place the intake as close to the bottom as possible.

Choosing Your Fan Size

Fans are rated in either cubic feet (CFM) or cubic meters per minute in North America. That means a 70 CFM fan will move 70 cubic feet of air in one minute. Your fan should be big enough to move the volume of your grow room two to three times every minute. For example, a 70 CFM fan would be adequate for a 35 cubic foot area and would be optimal for roughly a 23 cubic foot area.

To figure out your area's cubic volume, multiply (in feet) the length by the width by the height. Since all exhaust fans are rated in CFM, all you need to do is calculate your room size, multiply it by three and find a fan rated slightly higher than this number.

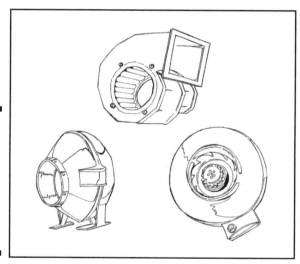

Figure 5-5: Determine where you can mount your fan before you decide which type to buy.

Installing your exhaust fan

Your exhaust fans should be placed at the far end of your grow room and away from the air intake source. If the fan can be mounted, it should be placed near the top of the grow room so that the hottest air is removed from the area first.

As with your air intake fan and oscillating fans, you can choose to run it 24 hours a day, only when the lights are on, or connected to a sophisticated release timer. If you don't have the means or access to one of these timers, it is recommended that you run your exhaust fan while your lights are on and for at least an hour after they turn off.

The fan is actually lowering the air pressure inside the area. Any incidental pinholes or leaky seams will simply draw air in. If the fan were blowing IN, those pinholes and leaks would allow potentially smelly air OUT.

Adjusting light timer cycles

If you find that the "lights off" temperatures are lower than they should be for optimum plant growth, you can simply run the fan from the same timer as the light by using a multi-outlet power strip connected to the timer. Plug the lights and the fan into the power strip and the fan will turn on and off with the lights.

If you're using more than one fan, you could connect some or all of them in this configuration, remembering that the more fans you have running, the lower the temps will be. Before you connect more than one device to a timer, make sure the timer can handle the additional electrical load or additional timers must be used.

Temperature

To make sure you're providing the right thermal environment for you plants through ventilation, oscillating fans, etc., you need to understand the physical nature of the heat in grow spaces, how it should be measured, and possibly adjusted.

Both excessively high and low temperatures can slow marijuana's rate of metabolism and growth. Cannabis plants function best in moderate temperatures — between 70 and 85°. As more light and/or CO_2 are made available, the ideal temperature for normal plant growth increases. In high temperature and moderate light conditions, the plant's stems elongate. Strong light and low temperature conditions will decrease stem elongation, which is preferred.

Hot Lamps

The high-pressure gas lamps used for cultivation can cause a considerable amount of heat build-up in an enclosed grow space. Obviously, excessive heat can be damaging to your plants.

The first thing to consider regarding the heat produced by HID lighting is the distance the lamp is from the tops of the plants. Under most circumstances a 1000-watt lamp with no shield should be kept no less than two feet from the top of the canopy. A 600-watt lamp can be placed as close as fifteen inches. A fluorescent tube of any wattage can be placed about six inches from the top of the plant.

The lamps also warm the air in the room. This heat must be discharged through the ventilation system. Cannabis seems to grow best at a temperature of 70° to 85°F. The temperature should not be allowed to rise any higher in grow rooms where no CO_2 enrichment takes place. When working with bottled CO_2, or even a CO_2 controller, the temperature can 85-95°F.

A temperature of approximately 65-70°F is ideal for darkness. In order to maintain an optimal temperature, you need an exhaust fan. The exhaust fan has a double function: refreshing the air and removing the heat. As described earlier, the capacity has to be great enough to replenish the air content of the grow room at least three times every hour. Also remember that when working at higher temperatures (by adding CO_2), the plant will need additional nutrient applications and more frequent reservoir refills.

Measuring Temperature

The standard mercury bulb or digital thermometer is designed to measure the temperature of the air. This is what is being referred to in the usual growers "rules of thumb" such as maintaining your grow above 70°F and below 85°F.

Most thermometers are only designed to measure air temperature. Growers often mistakenly place their thermometer in direct light, causing radiant energy to warm your thermometer and give a higher than actual reading.

Assuming your air is well mixed up by oscillating fans, it doesn't really matter where you locate your thermometer. The best spot is probably about half the way up a wall with a piece of cardboard over it to shade it from radiant heat. The thermometer should be exposed to the mixed air in the grow room and not a stagnant pocket in a corner of the room.

Extreme Light Intensity and Temperature

Cannabis loves high light levels/high radiant energy levels, but exceeding their tolerance for light can result in light burn and chlorophyll leaching out of the leaves. 600 and 1000-watt lamps put out a lot of light and in some circumstances, light burn can damage your clones and young plants.

To identify light burn damage, you should monitor your plants for leaves that look pale green (the edges may turn upwards), then turn yellow, and finally yellow/brown as the leaves scorch. Often you can see a circular pattern of intense light where the reflector has focused the light onto the plants. If plants outside of this intense light zone look greener and healthier, consider raising your lights.

Keeping the right temperature

Gardens using artificial lighting can generate high air temperatures. Each 1000-watt metal halide and ballast emits just a little less energy than a 10-amp heater. During the winter, the heat produced may keep the room comfortable. However, the room may get too warm during the summer and several lights can raise the temperature to an intolerable level.

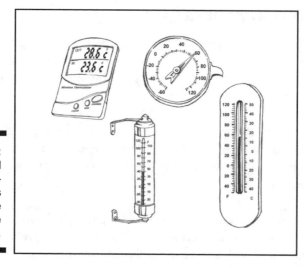

Figure 5-6:
Digital thermom-
meters
are more
accurate
and reliable.

Lowering grow room temperature

By far the most efficient method of eliminating heat, enabling the lights to be placed closer to the plants, is by using air-cooled lights. The lights are enclosed by the reflector, which holds a glass plate that captures most of the lamp's heat. Using four inch ducting powered by an inline fan, the lights draw in cool air from outside of the grow room to cool the light. Heated air is pushed out through the exhaust duct on the other side of the reflector. This air has never been in contact with the garden; it has no odor, just heat. It can be used to heat a space or just vented to the outdoors.

The advantage with this setup is that you're using less energy to move the heat out. The volume of air in the reflector might be three cubic feet and you can vent it out in a few seconds. It doesn't matter if it's hotter, just how much of it you have to move. Venting a 288 cubic foot grow room that's 95° takes a lot longer than venting a three cubic foot reflector that's 150°.

The least expensive way of reducing the heat in the grow room is to vent out the heat and replace it with cooler air. The previous sections of this chapter describe several methods for removing heated air and replacing it with fresh, cool air.

An expensive (but effective) way of reducing heat in the grow room is to use an air conditioner to maintain a specified temperature. There are many reasons why you should avoid using an air conditioner including its effects on the environment, the added expense on your electric bill, the cumbersome installation, and added noise. The only good reason to consider an air conditioner is simple, you've tried everything else and you have no choice.

Raising grow room temperature

Temperatures below 50° will slow growth in most varieties of marijuana. When the temperature drops below 40°, the plants may experience some damage and require 24 hours or more to resume normal growth. Low nighttime temperatures may delay or prevent bud maturation. Some equatorial varieties (Sativa strains) stop growing after a few 40° nights.

Overall, marijuana is low-temperature tolerant. Outdoors, seedlings sometimes pierce snow cover, and older plants can withstand short, light frosts. Low temperatures, however, slow down the rate of plant metabolism. Cold floors can lower the temperature in nutrient solution reservoirs, thereby lowering root temperature and slowing germination and plant growth. Ideally, the nutrient solution temperature should be around 68°.

There are several ways to warm the nutrient solution. The floor can be insulated using a thin sheet of Styrofoam, foam rubber, wood or newspaper. The best way to insulate a reservoir from a cold floor is to raise the container so that there is an air space between it and the floor. Overhead fans, which circulate the warm air downward from the top of the room, also warm the nutrient solution.

When the plants' roots are kept warm, the rest of the plant can be cooler without danger. Heat cables or heat mats, which use small amounts of electricity, can be used to heat the reservoir and nutrient solution. These are available at nursery supply houses.

Humidity

Humidity is the amount of water vapor present in the air. The humidity level affects the transpiration rate (the release water and waste) of the plant's stomata. When humidity is too high (moist air), the plants' stomata close, causing plants to transpire slowly and inhibiting growth. When humidity is too low (dry air), the plants' stomata open, causing plants to transpire too quickly, resulting in extremely narrow and paper-thin leaves that try to prevent excess water loss. Ideally, you want to maintain a level of humidity that allows your plants to evaporate water at a consistent, optimal rate. A mildly humid environment with a relative humidity of 40-60% is recommended.

WEED WARNING

If your grow room has too little humidity, your plants will dry out very quickly and will require more frequent watering. If your grow room has too much humidity, your plants could experience mold during the flowering phase. Realistically, humidity levels must be severely too high or too low to have a serious detrimental effect on your plants.

Plants grown in an arid (dry) environment may experience chronic wilt and necrosis of the leaf tips. Plants growing in a humid (wet) environment usually experience fewer problems. However, in a humid environment, buds are more susceptible to molds which can attack a garden overnight and ruin a crop. All mold, algae, spider, mite, aphid, whitefly, and fertilizer problems are reduced with proper ventilation.

Lowering Humidity

Growers are rarely faced with too dry a growing area. However, noticeable humidity (moist air) in your room is not healthy. It means you have inadequate airflow causing plants to draw only small portions of water while struggling to breathe from a lack of fresh carbon dioxide.

Since your grow space is enclosed, water that has evaporated or transpired by your plants will increase the room's humidity considerably. If there is no ventilation, a large space may reach saturation level within a few days. Smaller spaces usually don't have as much of a buildup because there is usually enough air movement to dissipate the humidity.

If you feel that your grow room is too humid even with adequate circulation and ventilation, you should consider using a dehumidifier. Dehumidifiers work the same way a refrigerator does except that instead of cooling a space, a series of tubes is cooled causing atmospheric water to condense.

The smallest dehumidifiers (which can dry out a large space) use about 15 amps. Usually the dehumidifier needs to run only a few hours a day. If the plant regimen includes a dark cycle, then the dehumidifier can be run when the lights are off, to ease the electrical load. Try putting a dehumidifier where your air comes in to take moisture out of the air as it enters your grow room.

Humidity for Seedlings

Humidity is also critical during germination and cloning when the seedlings and cuttings are extremely fragile. Humidity should be kept high at this phase to prevent the growing medium from drying too fast and to enable seedlings and cuttings to retain the small amount of nutrients they have available to them.

Chapter 6

Hydroponic Systems

· ·

In This Chapter

▶ Exploring hydroponic concepts

▶ Getting to know the different types of hydroponic systems

▶ Selecting the right medium for your system

▶ Maintaining your system and medium

· ·

There are numerous different types of hydroponic systems suitable for marijuana cultivation. Choosing the "best" system will depend on your individual growing environment and expectations. Some systems are better for growing large plants, as in a large closet grow, while others are best suited to growing smaller plants, like those using a Sea of Green (SOG) technique in a stealth environment.

For example, you probably would not consider NFT (Nutrient Film Technique) if you intended to grow your plants six feet high, since the NFT system is designed primarily for smaller crops. To grow a larger plant, you would likely be interested in a drip or ebb and flow system. On the other hand, NFT is an excellent choice for SOG growers.

Hydroponics offers you a vast opportunity for creativity. Most systems are relatively easy to build for an average do-it-yourselfer. By building your own system, you can save a lot of the initial investment, although you will still want to buy quality components. You can combine features of systems that best suit you and your growing situation. Or you can buy any of these systems complete from hydroponic manufacturers if you don't have the time to build your own. Complete systems are commercially available and contain everything you need. Some of the systems are very good quality and can potentially last for years.

Choosing a System

Take your time and give some thought to what you want to achieve with your garden. Read about the various types of hydroponic systems available before making a commitment. Check the discussion boards on the Internet for even more ideas. A little planning ahead of time will assure you of a successful garden the first time around.

WEED WARNING

Some hydroponics systems that are not suitable for growing marijuana are not included in this book. Very small NFT, vertical, bag culture, and passive hydroponic systems are ideal for smaller-type crops, but not for any form of marijuana, so they have been intentionally left out.

Drip

Drip systems are probably the most widely used type of hydroponic system in the world. Operation is simple: a timer controls a submersed pump which sends nutrient solution to the base of each plant by a small drip line. The excess nutrient solution that runs off is collected back in the reservoir for re-use.

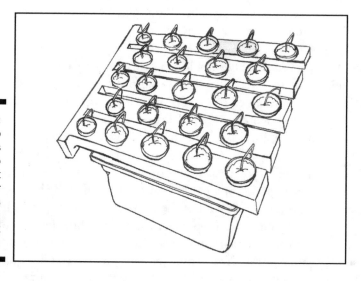

Figure 6-1:
Drip systems allow you to easily adjust the number of feedings depending on plant size.

A recovery system uses nutrient solution more efficiently, as excess solution is reused, this also allows for the use of an inexpensive timer because a recovery system doesn't require precise control of the watering cycles. A recovery system can have large shifts in the pH and nutrient strength levels that require periodic checking and adjusting.

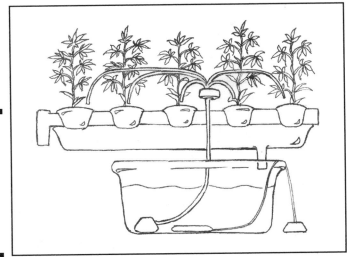

Figure 6-2:
Growing media should be flushed periodically as excess nutrients build up.

Ebb and Flow

The Ebb and Flow system works by temporarily flooding a grow tray with nutrient solution and then draining the solution back into the reservoir. This action is normally done with a submerged pump that is connected to a timer.

When the timer turns the pump on, nutrient solution is pumped into the grow tray. When the timer turns the pump off, the nutrient solution flows back into the reservoir. A timer is set to turn on several times a day, depending on the size of the plants, temperature, humidity, and the type of growing medium used.

The Ebb and Flow is a versatile system that can be used with a variety of growing medium. The entire grow tray can be filled with Grow Rocks, gravel or granular Rockwool. Many people like to use individual pots filled with growing medium, which makes it easier to move plants around or even move them in or out of the system.

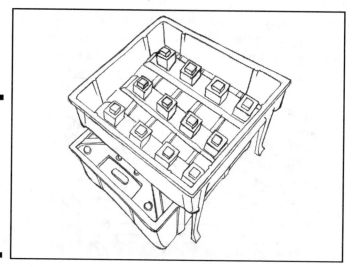

Figure 6-3:
Ebb
and flow
systems
require a
lot of trust
if you are
not able
to observe
them daily.

The main disadvantage of this system is that with some growing media such as gravel, grow rocks, and Perlite, there is a vulnerability to power outages as well as pump and timer failures. The roots can dry out quickly when the watering cycles are interrupted or the tank becomes empty. This problem can be relieved somewhat by using growing media that retains more water such as Rockwool, Vermiculite, coconut fiber or a good soilless mix.

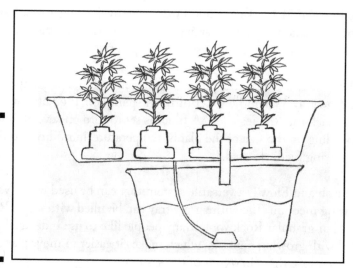

Figure 6-4:
Using
individual
pots can
help
increase the
sturdiness
of your
plants.

Aeroponic

Aeroponics is a hydroponic technique involving the use of sprayers, nebulizers, foggers, or other devices to create a fine mist of solution to deliver nutrients to plant roots.

In many aeroponic systems, the plant roots are suspended above a reservoir of nutrient solution or inside a channel connected to a reservoir. A pump delivers nutrient solution via sprayer nozzles, which then drips or drains back into the reservoir. Aeroponic systems are favored over other methods of hydroponics because the increased aeration of nutrient solution delivers more oxygen to plant roots, stimulating growth and preventing algae formation.

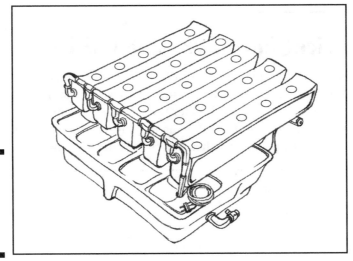

Figure 6-5:
Aeroponic systems can be tricky, but are worth the effort.

A variation of the technique employs the use of nebulizers or foggers instead of spray nozzles to deliver nutrient solution. This technique is considered even more effective, as it reduces the solution to extremely small particles which are readily absorbed by plant roots. It encourages development of a healthy plant root system, whereas with traditional aeroponics the roots can become matted and bound.

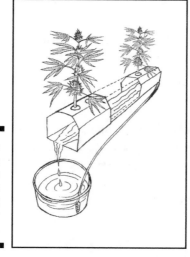

Figure 6-6:
Misters
provide
roots with
an optimal
mix of water
and air.

Nutrient Film Technique (NFT)

This is the kind of hydroponic system most people think of when they think about hydroponics. NFT systems have a constant flow of nutrient solution so no timer is required for the submersible pump. The nutrient solution is pumped into the growing tray (usually a tube) and flows over the roots of the plants, and then drains back into the reservoir.

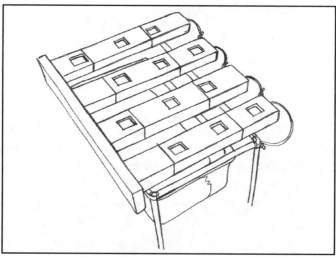

Figure 6-7:
NFT
systems
allow plants
to use the
nutrients
they need
as they
need them
without a
buildup.

There is usually no growing medium used other than air, which saves the expense of replacing the growing medium after every crop. Normally the plant is supported in a small plastic basket with the roots dangling into the nutrient solution.

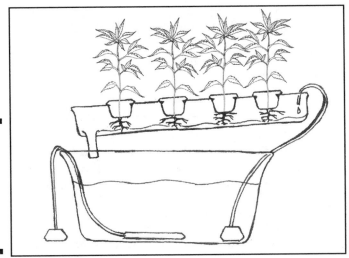

Figure 6-8:
A pump failure can ruin a entire crop in a day if it's not caught in time.

Basic Components

Regardless of which hydroponics technique/system you choose, each contains some of the same basic parts. The following sections describe the components so you will know what you are looking at when it comes time to build or buy.

❧ Reservoir (1)
In addition to lighting, the nutrient reservoir is the life force of your garden because it contains the water and nutrients your plants require for growth and maturation. Reservoirs are available in many sizes, but most are rectangular in shape. Complete "out-of-the-box" hydroponic systems are usually packaged with a reservoir that is appropriately sized for the number of plant sites it includes.

❧ Trays (2)
Hydroponic trays typically sit on top of the reservoir tank or are in some way elevated above it. Each tray holds some or all of the growing containers and active systems use these trays to collect run-off water and nutrients and guide them back into the reservoir for later use.

❦ **Plant containers** (3)

Most systems provide a growing container for each plant the hydroponic system was designed to grow. Store-bought systems indicate the number of plants they were designed to grow with and include the necessary hydroponic system components to grow that number of plants or less. Growing containers help determine the overall size of your plants, so you should consider this when choosing which system to purchase or build.

❦ **Tubing** (4)

Tubing is used to move water from the reservoir tank to the plants' growing containers where it can be absorbed by their roots. Tubing can also used to return unused water and nutrients back to the reservoir tank. Small tubing should be monitored for leaks and plugged with rubber sealant or even electrical tape.

❦ **Water pump** (5)

The majority of hydroponics systems use submerged, in-line water pumps. It's import to look for quality systems that include pumps designed specifically for rigorous use in hydroponic applications. Also ask about noise, efficiency, and replacement parts before choosing a system.

❦ **Timer** (6)

To supply water periodically to your plants, you need a timer with a minute setting that can switch on and off at least 6 times a day. Modern timer clocks are digital. These clocks have a memory to store the desired times. If the electricity goes off, batteries usually supply current to preserve the memory. Other timers use tabs, which can be pushed in or pulled out to determine on/off times.

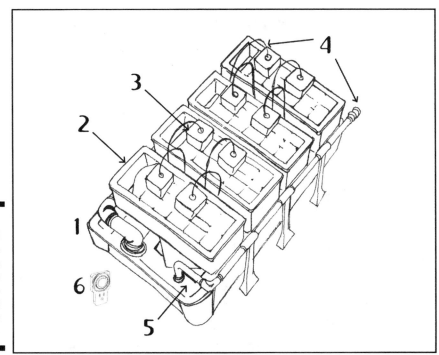

Figure 6-9:
Understand
how all the
components
work so you
know how to
troubleshoot
if problems
arise.

System Maintenance

Sterilizing and maintaining clean conditions inside your hydroponics and aeroponics systems is extremely important. Keeping cloning, vegetative and flowering systems clean gives your plants a fighting chance against pythium (root rot) and other harmful diseases, ensuring healthy and vigorous crops.

Failure to periodically clean a system can result in stressed plants becoming infected and rapidly spreading disease throughout the entire system. Once infected, the entire crop will experience reduced vigor and yield and ultimately crop failure.

Prevention is the best "cure" for disease. Routine disinfection, periodic sterilization, and attention to system design can help to combat diseases. The following are some procedures on how to keep your hydroponics system in good working order and suggestions on how often cleaning should be done.

Monthly Maintenance

1. Remove all plant matter from your system.

2. Pre-flush net cups/pots with hot water and inspect to ensure all roots have been removed. Put net cups/pots through dishwasher, then remove and soak in strong hydrogen peroxide (bleach is not recommended, as it leaves a toxic residue).

3. If infection was present, replace any grow medium; soak gro-rocks in strong hydrogen peroxide.

4. Optional: Remove and inspect all irrigation. Soak all tank accessories in strong hydrogen peroxide (misters too, if possible).

Note: Wear gloves when handling concentrated peroxide.

Post-Harvest Maintenance

1. Flush your system with water and do a pre-wipe using hot water and rubbing alcohol to remove salt and slime buildup on all system surfaces.

2. Disconnect your hydroponics system and lay it on a plastic tarp.

3. Mix up a very strong hydrogen peroxide solution (20%) and spray it onto all system surfaces and let it sit for at least a day.

4. Reconnect and run your system with 10% hydrogen peroxide and hot water for several hours.

5. Dump the cleaning solution and flush again thoroughly using fresh water.

6. Allow your system to sit for a day or two before planting any seedlings.

Growing Medium

Plants for most agricultural and horticultural crops are grown in the soil that nature provides. While fertilizer and organic materials may be added to improve plant growth, the basic growing medium is natural soil.

Marijuana cultivators who grow hydroponically have found that soil isn't the best medium to use for growing plants indoors. Other, soilless materials work better and are easier for them to manage in a hydroponic system.

The term **growing medium** can be defined as any substance that a plant's roots can grow and develop in. A growing medium must provide oxygen, water, nutrients and support for plant roots.

Hydroponic growers can use various soilless mediums such as water, gravel, coconut fiber, Rockwool, and many others to grow marijuana. The following sections discuss the types of hydroponic growing mediums and proper growing medium management.

Types of Medium

There are hundreds of different kinds of growing mediums; anything that a plant can grow in is considered a growing medium. There are man-made as well as organic (natural) mediums and even plain water can be an effective growing environment for roots.

Novice growers tend wonder which growing medium is the best. Unfortunately, there is no single growing medium that can be termed "the best" because the best medium for your situation depends on many variables. The type of system you are running, the growing technique you are using, and your local environment are just some of the many determining factors involved when choosing a growing medium. There may be several media that will work equally well for your particular needs. Many times it boils down to availability, price or personal preference.

Use the following list of the most popular types of growing mediums to help decide which types will work best for you. Each description includes details about general use, advantages and disadvantages, and particular characteristics of the growing medium.

Rockwool

Rockwool is one of the most popular growing mediums in the world because it retains moisture well, yet holds 18 % air as well, providing a healthy growing environment for the root system. Rockwool was originally used as insulation and was called "Mineral Insulation." It was developed for gardening in Denmark and is used extensively around the world for "Drip-Style" hydroponic systems.

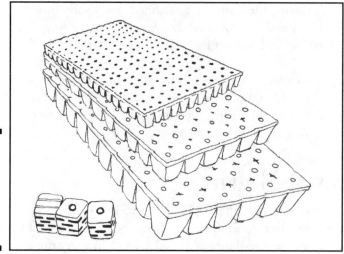

Figure 6-10:
Rockwool is an extremely versatile growing medium.

Rockwool is made by melting a combination of rock and sand and then spinning the mixture to make fibers that are formed into different shapes and sizes. Rockwool can vary in shape shapes from small starter cubes up to very large slabs, with many sizes in between. The vast range in available sizes makes Rockwool one of the most versatile growing mediums.

The advantages to Rockwool are many, however there are several disadvantages to this type of growing medium as well.

Advantages

☘ Retains Water
Rockwool holds an incredible amount of water, which gives you a "buffer" against power outages and pump (or timer) failure.

☘ Holds Air
Rockwool holds at least 18% air at all times (unless it is sitting directly in water), which supplies the root zone with plenty of oxygen. This means that it is practically impossible to over-water Rockwool.

☘ Available in a Variety of Sizes and Shapes
From small cubes designed for use in propagation to large slabs capable of holding the root systems of multiple plants, Rockwool comes in dozens of shapes and sizes making it a versatile growing medium. Rockwool also comes "loose" so you can fill pots or containers of any size.

✤ Clean and Convenient

Rockwool holds together very well so it can't spill. Rockwool also comes wrapped in plastic, which makes it easy to handle and keeps evaporation to a minimum.

Disadvantages

✤ Not Environmentally Friendly

Rockwool is hard to dispose of, if buried it will last indefinitely.

✤ Dust and Fibers are a Health Risk

The fibers and dust from the Rockwool are bad for your lungs. Wear a dust mask when handling to prevent problems.

✤ pH Problems

Rockwool has a high pH which means you have to adjust your nutrient solution low so that the root zone is neutral. Rockwool is also susceptible to pH shifts meaning a bit more routine maintenance to keep the pH levels correct.

✤ Long Pre-Soak Period

Rockwool must be pre-soaked for 24 hours before use. Most other growing medium only needs to be well watered.

Clay pellets

Expanded clay pellets, also know as grow rocks, are used as a lightweight replacement for gravel. The pellets do not absorb water and can be reused again and again after each crop has been harvest. Because of their small size, they are commonly used in conjunction with coconut fiber cups.

Expanded clay pellets are a man-made product created by baking clay in a kiln. The insides of the clay pellets are full of tiny air pockets, similar to lava rock, which makes it a lightweight medium. The pellets work well in hydroponics systems that have frequent watering cycles because the pellets don't retain much water and need to be watered often so that the plant roots won't dry out. The pellets are often mixed with other growing mediums to increase oxygen retention.

Expanded clay pellets can be expensive, but they are one of the few kinds of growing mediums that are easily reusable, which makes them a good choice for the long term. After you harvest your crop you can wash the clay rocks to remove all the old roots and then sterilize them with a 10% bleach to water mix.

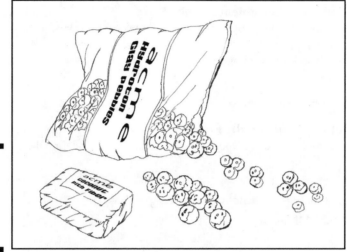

Figure 6-11:
Coconut
fiber is a
natural
alternative
to rockwool.

Coconut fiber

Coconut fiber is totally organic and retains more oxygen than Rockwool. This growing medium is very high in root stimulating hormones. Coconut fiber is made of the powdered husks of the coconut itself and is essentially a waste product of the coconut industry.

One of coconut fiber's many advantages is its capacity for holding oxygen while also having superior water holding ability. The dual capability can be an advantage for hydroponic systems that have intermittent watering cycles.

Coconut fiber is also high in root stimulating hormones and offers some protection against root diseases including fungus infestation. Dutch growers have found that 50% coconut fiber and 50% expanded clay pellets is a great mix to use as a growing medium for cannabis.

Soilless mix

Soilless mix is a combination of several different natural ingredients. These mixes contain a vast assortment of ingredients, but usually contain things like sphagnum moss, Vermiculite and Perlite. Soilless mixes are usually considered organic and have very fine particles that can clog pumps and drip emitters if you don't use a good filtration system.

Most soilless mixes retain water well and have great wicking ability while still holding a good amount of air, making them a good growing medium for a variety of hydroponic and organic gardens.

Water culture

Air is frequently used as a growing medium in aeroponic systems that have plant roots that hang in air and are periodically sprayed with a nutrient solution. The biggest advantage to growing in air is that the roots get all of the oxygen they could possibly need. Another major advantage is that it costs nothing and there are no disposal problems as with some other growing mediums.

Many aeroponic systems use net cups that hold a minimal amount of growing medium to stabilize the plant. Expanded clay pellets in coconut fiber cups are popular with these types of aeroponic systems.

Managing the Medium

WEED WARNING

After a period of time, a grow medium can tend to break down, medium-borne diseases microorganisms can build up, and old roots can take up more and more of the pore space. Because of these potential problems, growers must change or sterilize the growing medium to prevent possible problems. Poor sanitation can destroy an entire crop in a very short amount of time.

Soft, lower cost mediums (sawdust, peat mixes, etc.) may be changed after every crop to prevent possible growing problems. Even some of the more durable aggregates (clay pellets) may need to be changed periodically due to reduced pore space and the resulting excessive moisture retention.

Durable aggregates that will be used for more than one crop must be sterilized between crops to prevent possible disease problems. This is particularly important in closed growing systems such as ebb and flow systems.

Good sanitation is extremely important, especially in an indoor hydroponic environment. After a period of irrigation, toxic quantities of fertilizer salts may build up on the aggregate particles. Aggregates should be rinsed with clean water once every two weeks to help dissolve the accumulated salts.

Chapter 7

Water and Nutrients

. . . .

In This Chapter

▶ Understanding how plants use water and nutrients

▶ Measuring and adjusting water quality

▶ Selecting the right nutrients for different growing phases

▶ Supplying the optimum amount of nutrients

. . . .

Like all other forms of life, marijuana plants need water and specific nutrients to survive. Water used by the cannabis plant, as well as all other plants, has three functions: it is a building material (together with CO_2 and light energy, glucose is produced), it makes the plant sturdy (the plant cells fill themselves with water, giving the plant a firm structure), and it transports nutrients throughout the plant. Water is indispensable for the existence of plants.

When grown outdoors, marijuana plants pull water from the soil into the plant. The water is in the form of a natural "soup" that contains nutrients that the plants use to grow. In an outdoor grow, water is available naturally through rain and groundwater, but is often manually supplemented if possible. In most climates, the amount of water naturally available is sufficient for a thriving crop, but the amount of nutrients may be lacking.

When growing hydroponically, nutrients are mixed with water and placed in a reservoir, where a pump and tubing are used to feed the plants. The advantage over outdoor growing is that you can precisely control how much nutrient you provide your plants as well as how often. You also gain a cost advantage in that nutrients are re-circulated in the system, so you only have to provide "fresh" nutrients every week or two—the hydroponics system handles the rest of the work.

Water Basics

Osmosis is the processes in which plants absorb water and nutrients. Osmosis is based on the principle that a plant's root system is semi-permeable, meaning it's walls permit some materials to pass through, and others not. Osmosis enables the "hitch-hiking" of nutrients together with the water that are transported up into the plant's cells. These nutrients are necessary to allow the plant's growth processes to take place.

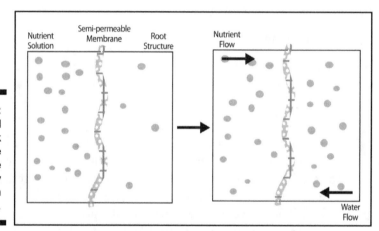

Figure 7-1:
Nutrients and water work through the membrane until they attain equilibrium.

Among other things, osmosis provides for the sturdiness in plants' cells. The osmotic process allows the plant to absorb so much water that the plant's cells become saturated, causing the stalk and the leaves stand upright. Conversely, if too little water is in supply, the plant cells transpire water. When a plant gives off water without replenishing it, the plant's strength is lost, and eventually the plant will wilt and die.

Another way for a plant to lose its sturdiness is for osmosis to work in the reverse direction. If the concentration of nutrients in the water fed to the plant is too high, the plant will not absorb water, but release it, and become less sturdy by drying out and burning. You can use a PPM meter, described later in this chapter, to measure and adjust nutrient concentration to the appropriate strength.

Water Quality

Bad water can cause big problems. Pure water is often not available to hydroponic growers. Almost all domestic water supplies contain certain "dissolved solids," minerals that cannot be filtered out in the way that particles can. Generally these conditions won't cause too much trouble. A simple pH adjustment will usually correct an imbalance caused by "hard" water.

Although tap water in most areas is highly chlorinated, this does not appear to harm marijuana plants. Countless fine crops are raised with water straight from the tap.

However, there is a limit. In some areas the amount of total dissolved solids or of specific elements in the water supply can combine with elements in the nutrient solution resulting in a form of nutrient lockout. This may occur when well water is used to mix nutrient solution or where the municipal water supply is very hard. Water containing more than 100 parts per million (PPM) of calcium and magnesium (called "total hardness") can create serious problems. Other common elements that may be present in hard water include various carbonates, sulfur, sodium, iron and boron.

Nutrient lockout happens when your plant can't access some or all of the nutrients in the growing medium. This is due to a chemical reaction within the medium/solution that prevents nutrients from being absorbed by the roots. The pH level of your nutrient solution is also a leading cause of nutrient lockout. Keeping your pH level within an acceptable range enables your plants to absorb the full range of nutrients it needs.

Nutrient lockout repair

For acute deficiency symptoms caused by toxicity and nutrient lockout administer the following first aid procedure:

Leach the plants roots and growing medium (using fresh, clean, pH adjusted water) to thoroughly leach away metals, calcium, sodium, chlorides, sulfates and many other compounds, which can build up in the growing media.

Feed with a ¼ strength high-quality nutrient mix along with a high quality vitamin B-1 product such as Super-thrive (one drop per gallon). Feed at ¼ of the recommended fertilizer dosage until first signs of growth.

Water temperature

High root zone temperatures often plague indoor growers running hydroponic systems. These systems are subject to rapid heating by intense HID lighting, which increases root zone temperatures and decrease dissolved oxygen (DO) levels. Rapid plant growth, combined with low DO levels, can cause oxygen deprivation. This deprivation can result in infection by opportunistic pathogens such as pythium.

The key to maximum growth is to keep the air temperature at 75-80°F and the root zone at 68°F. Significantly lower temperatures slow down the metabolism of the plant and its growth. On the other hand, higher temperatures will have less dissolved oxygen in the solution, causing the roots to be more vulnerable to diseases and pathogens. Maintaining nutrient temperatures at or under 68°F maximizes root growth.

pH Level Metering

The pH level of your nutrient solution is an important factor to monitor and maintain while growing marijuana. A lot of gardeners have trouble adjusting the pH of their solutions, so you should understand the basic fundamentals of how pH works before measuring and making adjustments.

The pH level of your nutrient solution is critical to enabling your plants to absorb the nutrients in your reservoir. A pH imbalance can stunt the growth of your plants and affect the yield of your harvest. The pH level of your nutrient solution is based on the acidity (pH) of the water and can be measured on a scale from 1 to 14. A solution with a pH between 1 and 7 is acidic, a pH of 7 is called neutral, and a pH between 7 and 14 is alkaline. The lower the pH, the more acidic the solution.

Generally for hydroponic applications, the recommended pH range for cannabis is between pH 5.5 and pH 6.2. If the nutrient solution should become more acidic or alkaline, the availability of certain nutrients would decrease, making nutrients less available or even completely unavailable to the plant. As your plants absorb nutrients and release waste material into the solution, the pH level naturally fluctuates, so it must be measured and continually adjusted.

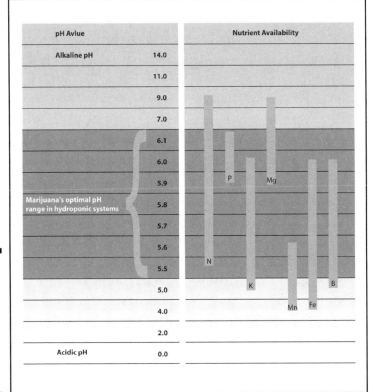

Figure 7-2: By maintaining an optimal pH level, your plants have full access to nutrients.

When you measure your nutrient solution and find that your pH level is out of the 5.5-6.2 range, you must manually adjust the solution back into range. You should test the pH level of your nutrient solution every day for the first days of a grow and then at least once a week, even if your plants look healthy. However, before you make any adjustments you must accurately measure your solution.

Types of Meters

The first step in determining if high pH is the real problem is to pick up a good pH tester. Don't be afraid to shell out the cash for a good one, its well worth it.

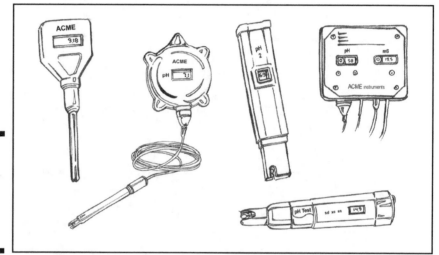

Figure 7-3:
Combo and waterproof meters can save you money in the long run.

Waterproof pens

Waterproof pens are available for measuring PPM, pH, or both and allow you to easily monitor your nutrient solution without fear of dropping it in the solution as most are waterproof and float as well. Some feature replaceable probes so the entire pen doesn't have to be tossed when the electrodes corrode. You may be able to purchase a standard pen that isn't waterproof and doesn't allow you to change the electrodes, but they aren't recommended.

Portable meters

These meters are designed to allow you to monitor your nutrient solution by briefly placing a probe into the nutrient solution to get a reading. Most are battery powered for portability. The better versions feature replaceable probes and a decent amount of cable between the probe and meter. These types of meters can also be used for continuous metering but are limited to the strength of their batteries.

Constant monitoring meters

These types of meters are designed to constantly monitor your solution so that you can always keep a reading on your nutrient solution. Standard features include a removable 12-volt power supply, replaceable probes, and a 6-foot cable between meter and probes. Some even use "set points" that allow you to set a knob to the ideal pH or PPM level and if your solution exceeds a set range, the meter alarm light turns on.

pH test strips

pH test strips are quick and easy to use. Just touch a strip to your nutrient solution and match the color of the strip to an included color chart. Results appear in seconds and you get about 100 strips per vial. This is an inexpensive metering solution, but the readings aren't as accurate as a digital meter.

pH test kit

The pH test kit will test the pH of your nutrient solution and give you an accurate reading for adjustment if necessary. It comes with a small bottle of indicator solution, vial, and color chart. These are also inexpensive and a little more accurate than test strips, but still give imprecise readings compared to digital meters.

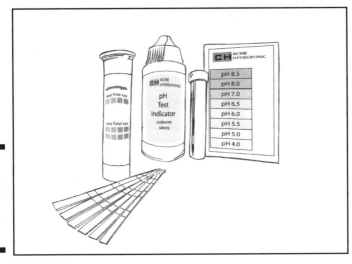

Figure 7-4:
Test strips and kits are inexpensive, but not very accurate.

Pen maintenance

You should recalibrate your pH and PPM meters about once a month. Some meters need a special storage solution for the sensor. Please be sure to buy this storage solution, it will make the difference between a well-working meter and a useless meter.

pH adjustment

When adjusting the pH level of a hydroponics system, your best bet is to use professional pH Up and pH Down solutions. Available in most grow shops in a range of sizes, these products allow more precise control over pH adjustment than the basic minerals used by many outdoor growers. The mixture of solution to water varies between brands, so make sure you read the label and understand the recommended dosage before you add it to your reservoir.

Figure 7-5:
A small amount of chemical adjustment can handle minor pH problems.

Always determine the growing medium pH using a pH test kit or meter before adding seeds or transplants and make sure it measure between 5.5-6.2. This simple rule can make the difference between an easy-to-handle garden and a persistent headache. If your pH falls out of this range, use a pH up or down solution found at garden supply stores.

Adjusting the pH can be maddening sometimes, because the scale is exponential. In practical terms, this means that you have to lower the pH or raise the pH by adding very small amounts of adjusters. If your pH is too high and you add too much pH down, you will have to add pH up. This can go on for while and then your nutrient solution strength might get be high.

To avoid these problems, use a syringe or a teaspoon to measure your solution before you put it into your reservoir. Also remember to check pH levels often as you adjust pH slowly over several days. Never adjust your pH level more than a full point while plants are in place. The severe hydrogen swing will shock the roots and imbalance the medium's micro flora and micro fauna.

Over Watering

Over watering is a common mistake of novice growers. Over watering can cause an imbalance in your precisely measured nutrient solution and your plants end up growing in a saturated mess. When plants are over watered, oxygen can't get to the roots and the entire plant suffers. The plants start to show similar symptoms of a plant that is dying from under watering.

Often, a novice grower sees the leaves going brown will continue to give it more water and fertilizer, not knowing that they are gradually giving it a massive overdose. If you find that you have been over watering your plants and can recognize your mistake in time, don't water your plants until the top 3–4 inches of the medium have dried out. Then, gradually reinvigorate your plants by feeding them pure fresh water that has been standing for 24 hours.

Under Watering

Brief under watering has a less long-term affect effect on the marijuana plant in comparison to over watering. When plants start to wilt, one of the first things you should check is the whether the plants have been receiving enough water and at appropriate intervals.

If you find that your plants are under watered, immediately water the plants again and go back to them an hour or two later. They should have picked up with no noticeable damage. Make sure that your timer, pump, hoses, emitters, etc., are all working properly without leaks, clogs of other malfunctions. Precise and consistent watering is a major factor in successful marijuana cultivation.

Regular visits to your grow room will help you understand your plants' water needs. Poke your finger two or three inches into the plant's growing medium. If the medium is moist and the plant looks healthy, upright, and strong, leave your watering schedule alone.

Figure 7-6:
Over-watering and underwaterig can appear similar, check the rooms to verify your diagnosis.

How can I tell if my plants are over watered or under watered?
Leaves that are drooping from under watering will look limp and lifeless. Leaves that are drooping from over watering will be firm and curled down, even from the stem of the leaf.

Nutrient Basics

As with all aspects of growing indoors, you have a lot of control over how you administer nutrients to your plants. However, you also have the greatest number of options when it comes to selecting what nutrients you supply, how often, and at what strength. Naturally, it's important to understand the relationship between the marijuana plant and the nutrients it needs in order to thrive.

There are hundreds, if not thousands, of fertilizers available for all different types of plants and growing situations, both indoor and out. However, if you plan to use a hydroponics system, your options are greatly limited. If you narrow your choice in nutrients to those designed specifically for hydroponic systems, you can easily pick up just a few different bottles of solution and be covered for all the different phases of plant growth.

Instead of learning about each nutrient in-depth, leave it to the experts who design nutrient solutions specifically for your purposes. The advantage in these solutions is that you rarely get nutrient deficiencies. If anything, you are more likely get nutrient lockout, which can be much easier to remedy by adjusting the pH levels of your nutrient solution.

The next few sections briefly cover the nutrients that a marijuana plant uses to grow and flower. You should at least understand the fundamentals so you know why you are buying different nutrient solutions for different phases and how their ingredients will affect your grow. Beyond the types of fertilizer you use, you will also learn how to measure and adjust the strength of nutrients that you apply. Finally, you will learn basic reservoir maintenance so your system lasts longer and your plants stay healthy.

Macro Nutrients	Micro Nutrients
(primary nutrients)	(Secondary nutrients)
Carbon (C)	Boron (B)
Hydrogen (H)	Chlorine (Cl)
Oxygen (O_2)	Copper (Cu)
Nitrogen (N)	Iron (Fe)
Phosphorus (P)	Manganese (Mn)
Potassium (K)	Zinc (Zn)
Calcium (Ca)	Molybdenum (Mo)
Magnesium (Mg)	
Sulfur (S)	

Most of the marijuana plant is formed from hydrogen, carbon and oxygen (95% of the dry mass). Carbon comes from carbon dioxide (CO_2) in the air. Hydrogen and oxygen come from water. Note that this oxygen must be available "mixed in the water," as dissolved oxygen.

The chemical composition of the nutrient solution is important. Without certain nutrients plants cannot live and cannot complete their life cycle. Toxic substances in the solution could cause the plant to die. With the plethora of nutrient products currently available to most growers, the nutrient composition is rarely a problem.

Labeling Explained

The first step in evaluating a fertilizer is understanding how the **N-P-K** numbers, nitrogen (N), phosphate (P), and potassium (K), are used to rate nutrient solutions. There are two ways to interpret these numbers: first, as a concentration, and second, as a ratio. Both methods are important to understand.

As a concentration, the numbers are the percentage, by weight, of the nutrients available to your plants. For example, in a one-gram sample of Mega-Gro 15-30-15, 15% (or 0.15 gram) would be available as nitrogen, 30% (0.30 gram) as phosphorus, and 15% (0.15 gram) as potassium. The 40% "missing" balance contains the remaining macro- and micro-nutrients, but it is mostly inert filler that does not affect plant growth.

A fertilizer labeled 7-15-7 would be about half the strength of a nutrient solution labeled 15-30-15. You could apply half as much of the stronger fertilizer to get the same nutrient strength as the weaker 7-15-7 fertilizer, but you could more easily burn your plants without properly diluting the stronger fertilizer.

Consider the N-P-K number as a ratio. In the case of a 15-30-15 fertilizer, the ratio would be 1:2:1. This means there is twice as much phosphorus than nitrogen or potassium in the fertilizer, although the ratio does not indicate the fertilizer's absolute concentration.

You want to grow vegetatively using more nitrogen than anything else and flower with more phosphorous than anything else. When switching over to flowering start by using half strength of the new nutrient solution and gradually increase to full strength to the vegetative nutrient strength.

Do chemical fertilizers affect how buds taste/smoke?
There is sometimes a common misconception that cannabis plants grown hydroponically using chemical fertilizer salts must have a chemical taste. This is certainly not the case and has been shown in research studies that hydroponically grown produce tastes no different than that which is grown in soil. Plants that aren't properly flushed or are cured incorrectly are thought to have a "chemical/hydro taste."

Plants that are hydroponically grown take up plant nutrients in exactly the same way as a plant does in the soil, no matter what the original source of nutrients (organic or inorganic) was. If you notice a difference in taste, it may be that you have not flushed or cured correctly.

Preformulated nutrients

A majority of successful indoor hydroponics growers are using a three or four-part solution that uses very high quality nutrient sources and is packaged in concentrated form to contain size and reduce shipping costs. These multi-part solutions usually list the actual dissolved elemental strength of your final solution, not just those misrepresentative N-P-K numbers as your only basis for determining elemental content.

Figure 7-7:
Multi-part
nutrients
give your
plants a
balanced
"diet" during
specific
growth
phases.

With some multi-part formulas, you are intended to use one part for each phase. Other formulas use a combination of two or more parts, with a different mix ratio for each phase of growth. These solutions typically consist of the following parts:

Microbase

A nitrate-based, chelated micronutrient solution. Also contains adequate N-P-K for general use. An excellent all around product for young clones or seedlings.

Part 1

A calcium nitrate-based solution for encouraging compact growth. This part supplies high levels of calcium, magnesium and nitrate form nitrogen.

Part 2

An ammonium nitrate-based solution for rapid development. Excellent for encouraging fast vegetative development and speeding up rejuvenation

Part 3

A potassium nitrate and potassium phosphate-based solution for excellent burning properties. This product supplies high phosphorous levels for blooming.

Recommended nutrient brands

Depending on your budget, you may want to start with the basic nutrient packs that are included with store-bought hydroponics systems. Just because they have been included doesn't mean they aren't any good. In fact, companies that manufacture hydroponic systems also produce nutrient solution, so they include free nutrients to "hook" you into their brand. The only problem is that the amount included isn't enough for even a single growing cycle and you'll soon need identical nutrients that may not be available at your local store.

You may want to find out which brands of nutrients are available to you through local hydroponics stores and then do a little research on the internet to find out how successful other growers have been in using them. Typically, if they are being stocked in the hydroponics store, people are buying them for good reason. You can then keep the freebie nutrients for emergency backup.

A lot of research has been devoted to advanced nutrient solutions and additives, with some companies concentrating specifically on improving nutrients for hydroponically grown marijuana. Unfortunately, some of the exciting new products emerging from this research are unavailable in most countries until they go through the proper trials and approval processes.

Because of bureaucratic red tape and because different areas have different brands available, it's impossible to recommend the "best" one. Choosing nutrients is one area where you need to do your own research and trial and error to find your own "best" nutrient solution. As long as you use multi-part solutions intended for hydroponic growing in the recommended dosage, your plants should flourish.

Nutrient Strength

Indoor gardeners can take advantage of their good growing conditions by supplying their crops with the right strength and formula of their nutrients as their crops grow. Use a good hydroponic nutrient designed for your growing medium—some fertilizers are mixed especially for soilless potting mixes, but they will not work well for crops growing in Rockwool. Use a vegetative growth nutrient solution until you shorten your light hours, then change to flowering or crop production nutrients.

With intense light levels, properly timed feedings, and good air movement already established in the garden, increasing food strength is worth considering. First, evaluate the growing conditions and the condition of the plants. If everything is going well, and plants are in a period of active growth, increase food strength gradually while carefully watching crops for signs of stress. Most growers are satisfied with reaching "full strength" level (800 -1600 PPM, depending on strain) by the end of their green growth period.

During the "transition" period — after shortening the day length, but before flowers begin to show — excessive growth is usually unwanted, and many gardeners actually reduce the strength of their fertilizer until their plants begin to show flowers.

Once plants are producing flowers, they are entering a period of active growth and increasing the strength of the nutrient mix can be very helpful. Do this carefully and gradually! Increase food strength by about 200 PPM, and then watch crops closely to be sure they are able to adjust to the stronger mix.

After a few days, if everything is going well, increase the strength of the nutrients again by the same amount. By carefully watching the plants to learn their reaction to the increased nutrient levels, growers can quickly learn what food strength is right for their plants and their garden.

Overfeeding

One of the most common problems for a beginning hydroponics grower is nutrient burn. It might look like a heat problem, but could also be a nutrient strength problem if the majority of leaves look affected. It's very rare that an inexperienced grower underfeeds his plants, but rather pumps up the nutrient strength in the belief that it helps the plants grow faster or produce a bigger yield.

The nutrient solution should not be too strong (over 1300-1600 PPM), nor should it be too weak. Each strain has is own preferred nutrient strength and it's far better to gradual increase the PPM of your solution until you find it rather than maxing it out and stunting the growth of your plants.

Nutrient Measurement

Dissolved solids (nutrients) can be measured by using an instrument called a conductivity meter. The higher the amount of dissolved solids the solution contains, the higher its conductivity will be. The conductivity meter measures the electrical conductivity in the solution and interprets that measurement in parts per million (PPM). Gauging the PPM level is the best method for measuring nutrient strength before and after adding nutrients to your reservoir.

It is critical that the nutrient solution not exceed the plant's tolerance for dissolved solids. That tolerance can range from extremely low for clones and seedlings to very high for plants in the flowering phase. When in doubt, remember that it is always better to apply too little nutrient than too much.

Parts Per Million (PPM) is a measurement of mass and determined by weighing, called a gravimetric analysis. A solution of nutrients dissolved in water at a strength of 700 PPM means that there are 700 milligrams of dissolved solids present for every liter of water.

PPM Meters

Total dissolved salts meters are essentially little voltmeters that look at the voltage produced by a sensor, usually a couple of metal pins. The nutrient solution acts like a battery electrolyte and the pins function like plates (electrodes) in a battery. The idea is that a nutrient solution is more electrically conductive when there are more nutrient salts in solution, so more salts means more voltage. A little math is done in the device to convert the voltage to PPM (parts per million of dissolved solids). It sounds complex, but all you need to know is that you need a meter that measures between 0-2000 PPM, which most do.

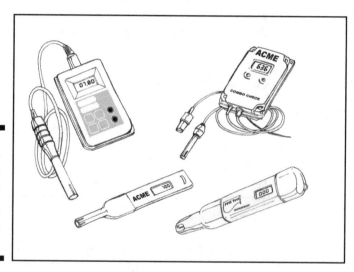

Figure 7-8:
Waterproof and continuous monitoring meters have the greatest lifespan.

There is a calibration adjustment on PPM meters, so it can be tweaked to compensate for various factors. You need a test solution to recalibrate your meter once a month. Usually you will use two tests solutions, one at 1500 or 1700 PPM and another at 0 PPM, which are used to verify that the meter is measuring accurately between these ranges.

PPM meters come in all of the same options as the pH level meters (pens, portable, waterproof, etc.), with the exception of the manual pH strips and test kits. Your only option for finding out your nutrient solutions PPM is by using a digital meter. Some meters are available in combination units, but the cost savings is small. If you choose to buy a combo unit, consider one that lets you replace the probes when they eventually malfunction.

Growing Medium Moisture

Growers that let their medium dry out to the point that leaves droop, greatly reduce their final yields and quality. The medium contains a certain amount of salts that dramatically increase in concentration as the water dissipates. Roots get stressed going through repetitive wet/dry cycles because the plant is being deprived of moisture that would normally be available for additional growth.

One way to monitor the moisture levels of your growing medium is to use a moisture meter. Simple, single-probe moisture meters are available at most garden centers for under $20 and don't use batteries. These meters can be invaluable for determining watering schedules, over watered conditions, and uneven moisture distribution within a plant's container.

Using a moisture meter is far more accurate than lifting the container and guessing because the weight of the container doesn't indicate where the moisture is inside. A grower would never really know if the bottom of the container was over saturated without a probe indicate it.

Measuring Moisture Levels

The moisture meter's probe should be inserted to various depths to accurately assess conditions. All moisture meters use a scale to indicate moisture levels, but what's important is relative moisture. The lower potion of the medium in the container should not be so consistently and constantly moist as to "bury the needle" at the top of the scale. The middle depths of the container should be kept in the upper half section of the meter's range and the top should be allowed to dry out to the lower half of the range before re-watering.

Topping Off

Reservoir maintenance is the routine task of keeping the hydroponic nutrient solution in the reservoir from becoming too strong or toxic as water evaporates and the plants absorb nutrients from the solution. In the course of operating a hydroponics system, two problems can occur with the water and nutrients in your reservoir:

As water evaporates out of the reservoir, the concentration of total dissolved salts (nutrients) in the solution gradually become stronger to the point of being toxic to the plants. The total dissolved salts will become stronger when water evaporates and fresh water is not replenished.

Hydroponically grown plants take up nutrients as they need them from the nutrient solution. A nutrient solution left alone will end up lacking key nutrients, with a build-up of toxic levels of other key nutrients.

The only way around these problems is to practice sound reservoir "topping off" procedures. The most widely accepted maintenance method involves weekly topping off and routine reservoir solution replacement. Once a week, you'll want to re-fill the reservoir with plain water and add nutrients if necessary.

Every other week, you should empty the entire reservoir and replace it with fresh water and fresh nutrients. This gives the plants a fresh and well-balanced nutrient solution, which has not been altered by the plants' nutrient uptake.

Plants grown hydroponically can harm themselves with nutrient deficiencies, lockouts and overdoses, if they are allowed to feed without some oversight on their "food bowl."

Chapter 8

Putting it all Together

In This Chapter

▶ Electrical safety tips

▶ Hanging your wall coverings

▶ Protecting your floor

▶ Placing fans and ducting

▶ Installing HID lighting

By now you should have already decided where to grow your crop and bought all of the necessary equipment for your grow room. The following chapter explains some of the tips and security issues you should familiarize yourself with as you get your room ready for its first grow.

If the space is confined, like a closet, it's important that you install your equipment in a certain order to make it as easy as possible. For instance, you might find it difficult to set up your hydroponics system if a large HID lamp is hanging in the way. Typically, you will want to start the bottom of your grow room and work your way up. This means that your hydroponics system is installed before your fans and your fans are installed before the lighting and so on.

The following sections are arranged according to the order you should install your equipment. The first section deals with electricity and works its way up from there.

Preparing the Room

Before you move equipment into your grow room, you should make sure the room is empty and completely enclosed. Start by removing anything in the grow space that does not involve growing. Most importantly, remove any clothes, drapes, or furniture that might introduce fungi and pests to your plants.

Once the room is cleared, it's time to vacuum, mop, scrub, dust and whatever else it takes to make the area spotless. Finally, use some disinfectant over every surface in the room. Cleaning can be a lot of work, but it helps eliminate a lot of problems before you start growing.

Enclosing the Room

An enclosed room makes it easier to control what goes on in your garden and easier to figure out what's going wrong. It's also essential to keep natural light out of your grow space during your plant's "dark period," because it affects your harvest. On the flip side, you also don't want light getting out of the space to curious eyes. To accomplish all these goals, you need to seal openings, windows, doors, vents, cracks, and anything else that allows light to get in or out.

If you are using a closet, an entire room, or a grow box, then there isn't much left to enclose other than the door and possibly the windows. Cover these openings discreetly so they don't look boarded up from the outside. Wherever you have decided to grow, use masking tape, foam rubber, weather stripping, and poster board to cover every little crack and opening.

After you have installed your grow light, turn it on at night and look at your grow space from the outside. If you see light "leaking" out, go back inside the room and seal it off. Either the room is completely enclosed or it's not. Keep sealing the room off until it's unnoticeable in the dark.

If you are using the corner of a basement or garage or a section of a larger closet, then you have to create false walls to completely enclose your grow space. Most growers use plywood sheeting, or black polysheeting to partition the growing area from everything else. The materials and the quality of work should be determined by how secure you want to make your grow space. If you're working in the deep recesses of a basement that nobody ever sees, then a few pieces of plywood should do the job. If you are working out of a space that sees a lot of nearby foot traffic, you need to invest the time and money to make it look unnoticeable from outside the room.

Grounding your Electrical Equipment

One of the frequently overlooked considerations of an indoor grow space is electrical safety. Although this topic covers many possible problems, the first one we deal with is proper grounding.

The most important part in wiring your grow room is a good ground connection. Transient electrical currents can occur when a bare wire or terminal screw touches a metal component of your system. Transient currents will travel through the path of least electrical resistance. If you have your ground wire terminated to the metal part of a component and the other end spliced to the ground of your three wire power supply, then the current will follow that path instead of going through your body.

WEED WARNING

Another consideration is that water greatly reduces a body's resistance, so if you have water all over your floor or your hands and feet, then you are increasing your chance of electrocution and possible death.

Electrical Safety Tips

🌿 Make sure that all electrical products are unplugged before servicing.

🌿 Keep all electrical wires off the floor and out of the way to avoid electrical shocks due to unwanted flooding or accidentally tripping over them.

🌿 The capacitors used in high intensity lighting carry an electrical charge even after being unplugged. Make sure to always use a rubber protection cap so not to accidentally touch the terminals.

- ☙ When using multiple HID lighting systems, use an individually breakered timer panel to avoid over loading the main circuit and tripping the main breaker.

- ☙ Do not put the ballast on anything flammable, even if mounted in a safety box. The ballast generates a high amount of heat and can easily cause a fire if it comes into contact with combustibles.

- ☙ Don't ever hang lights from their electrical cords. Hanging lights by the cord can cause connections to separate and short out. Always use a chain attached to hood of the reflector and securely fasten it to the ceiling or something stable over your hydroponics system.

- ☙ When adjusting the time on an industrial timer, always shut the power off before opening the timer.

Hanging your Wall Covering

Before you move any equipment into your room, you should cover the walls with a reflective wall covering. The following method is a very effective and economic system for hanging your wall covering. Using this method, you can hang reflective material like Mylar without risk of damage from tacks or staples. Using Velcro to hang your Mylar will also allow you to clean it with less risk of damage. Velcro also allows you to re-adjust your Mylar as often as necessary with ease.

If you plan to paint the walls with flat white paint or install false walls covered with reflective material, you can skip this section, but you should still install the covering before any other equipment.

1. Cut the sheet of Mylar to the desired shape and size. Keep your Mylar as clean as possible because it attracts dust and other particles.

2. Cut ½ inch square of Velcro and remove the protective paper from both sides.

3. Apply one Velcro square to each corner of your Mylar sheet using the self-adhesive backing.

4. Once the Velcro has been applied to each corner of your Mylar sheet, grasp the sheet with both hands and apply to the wall. Don't worry about getting it straight in this step.

5. Once the Mylar sheet has been applied, you can begin to straighten the sheet by pulling each corner tight, one at a time, and by reattaching the Velcro squares.

Additional Tips:

⚜ Purchase a roll of Velcro to save money.

⚜ Washing your hands prior to working with Mylar will eliminate much of oils on your skin, which can smudge shiny new Mylar. Using gloves will eliminate this problem.

⚜ Use a tape measure to measure and mark your Mylar sheets prior to cutting, you will cut much straighter sheets.

Protecting your Floor

Whether you are growing in a high-rise apartment building, growing in your closet, or even using the basement, you should protect your floor from water damage. Reservoirs can crack or drip tubes may become misaligned and drip on the floor. Even more common than that is leaving a water hose running to your reservoir. Once the reservoir is full, the excess water pours out onto the floor, creating a mess and possibly a lot of damage.

A little pre-planning before you actually install and set up your hydroponics system can prevent or entirely eliminate the possibility of water reaching your floor. The most basic preventative measure is to buy a waterproof drop cloth like the ones used by painters. These will protect your floor from small leaks and spills, but not much else. The best option is to buy a cheap children's pool from a toy store, preferably one that doesn't inflate. Other than to swim in, they are perfectly designed to contain a hydroponics reservoir. Now, no matter what happens to your big tank of water and nutrients, the furthest they could spill would be the kiddie pool. If a large water spill occurs, you can drain the pool by using a wet/dry vacuum.

Placing your Circulation Fan

To place the oscillating fans, you can mount some platforms to the walls. As mentioned in the Fans chapter, two fans is an absolute minimum. You need one fan to move air above the canopy of leaves, so place it high. The other fan is placed just above the hydroponic trays and slighting below the tops of your plants. This fan doesn't have to be as strong as the one above it as long as it prevents the air underneath from standing still.

Some smaller oscillating fans are built to be mounted directly onto the small using only a few screws. If you bought this type of fan, you can skip the shelves and you can also adjust the placement of your fans throughout your grow with less damage to the walls.

Configuring Fans and Ducting

While it's been heavily stressed how important it is to bring fresh air into your grow space, you also have to be careful about what to do with the air you are venting out of the room. Local and federal police agencies use thermal imaging devices to detect unusual heat signatures coming from homes. This is unlikely in most neighborhoods but if you live in an urban environment, you will want to take great care of where this expelled air ends up.

Safely exhausting hot air can be difficult. Law enforcement in your area may look for unusual heat emissions coming from opened windows, chimneys, dryer vents and other handy places. Running exhaust to outside sheds, barns and tree stumps is also well know to law enforcement officers. The following suggestions may give you some ideas on what to do with all that hot air.

> ☘ **Exhaust down the Sewer**
> Every house has a sewer vent standpipe. By venting down the sewer, the smell will be distributed amongst you and your neighbors. The sewer cleanout access is often a 3-way 4" ABS "T" with a threaded cap somewhere in the basement. Remove the cap, and hook your vent fan to the T (a 4-inch to 3-inch adapter funnel may be required) and run your fan 24/7. This will not affect normal use of the sewer.

🌿 **Exhaust up through the Attic**
A quality reflector provides superb light distribution and uniformity of light over the crop. Reflectors can increase available light by up to 30 percent and can double or even triple the total growing area. There are many types of light reflectors and choosing the appropriate one for your situation is another key factor in assembling your room.

🌿 **Carbon Filter**
A commercial carbon filter is usually made of metal and contains an advanced activated carbon with excellent odor absorption properties. The filter is placed either in the growing area, attached to the exit fan, or outside the growing area, connected by ducting to the growing area. All air exiting the growing area must therefore pass through the filter, which removes over 99% of odor and associated particles. If odor is your main concern regarding exhausted air, there are more options available and are fully described in the Security chapter.

Hanging Your Lights

Before you install your lights, make sure you have a working fire extinguisher in your grow area and preferably another one somewhere in your house. They are always good to have around for peace of mind and insurance in case something goes horribly wrong. Try to find an extinguisher that is made specifically for electrical fires.

As mentioned above, when installing your lighting, correctly assess the amount of electrical current you will need. 80% of the capability of your circuit breaker is the maximum draw you can safely extract from your electrical service. You cannot draw more current than your wires and fuse box/circuit breakers can handle. You must use proper equipment, strong modern wiring, and safety-approved and installed circuit breakers. These lights are on eighteen hours a day and the more lights you have, the more wear, heat, and pressure your system must handle. Any weakness from your circuit box, wires, and receptacles can cause overload (and the shutdown of your system) or worse, fire and actual endangerment of your grow system, your home, and possible your family.

Have a fire and smoke alarm in your grow room, one that is clearly audible in any part of your house. Try to get one that is not heat-sensitive, as your room temperature will be higher than normal (although ventilation should keep it within reasonable limits).

Horizontal Placement

The majority of light originates from the sides of the reflector, which are parallel with the bulb. This can be determined by looking at the pattern of light shining on the walls and floor. The sides of the reflector are angled and on many hoods the light footprint can be easily adjusted to suit your requirements. So remember, if you have a rectangular garden, it is important to position the longest side of the reflector parallel to the shortest side of your garden.

Figure 8-1:
Proper alignment of the light to your grow room ensures greater distribution of light.

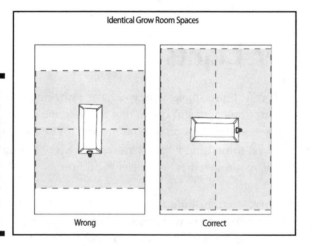

Vertical Placement

High wattage lights put out a lot of heat. Therefore, you should hang them far enough away from your plants so they don't burn. For example, 1000-watt lights should not be any closer than two feet from the tops of the plants.

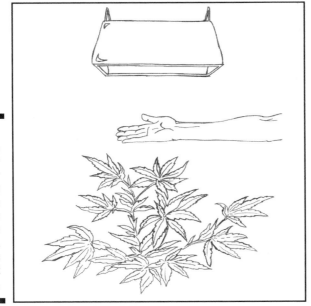

Another factor is how large the coverage area is; if you need a larger grow area then you should raise the light. Doing this will increase the coverage area, but decrease the intensity of the light. Light intensity decreases exponentially with distance from the plants, so the lights should be as close to the plants as possible without causing heat damage to the foliage.

Table 8-1	Light Mounting Heights	
Lamp Wattage	**Coverage Area**	**Mounting Height**
250w	2 x 2	1'
400w	3 x 3	1.5'
600w	3.5 x 3.5	2'
1000w	4 x 4	2.5'

Environmental conditions can also have an effect on lamp placement. Good ventilation and circulation keeps air moving around the foliage, which brings the temperature down and reduces the chance of heat damage. Under the right conditions, HID fixtures can be kept as close as six inches from the plants. However, in general, they should be kept twelve to eighteen inches away.

Start with your HPS about a foot away. If you see any signs of damage to the foliage, move it up to eighteen inches. If not, you can move it a little closer each day until you see your plants starting to suffer from the heat, then ease it back until you get the most intense light to your plants without causing damage.

Fluorescent lighting is much cooler and less intense than HID lighting, so plants should be kept very close to, almost touching, the bulbs.

Chapter 9

Grow Room Security

. . . .

In This Chapter

▶ Keeping a low profile

▶ Protecting your grow room

▶ Controlling and eliminating odor

▶ Concealing your grow room

. . . .

For some growers, their garden is their pride and joy. If you've put a lot of effort into your grow room and produced some of the finest marijuana you've ever smoked, you deserve to be proud. Unfortunately, because it's illegal almost everywhere, you need to keep your pride to yourself and it can be one of the hardest things to do for a beginning grower.

You might think that it's no big deal to show your best friends your thriving marijuana garden. But, your friend might tell his friend who might tell his friend until the wrong "friend" has information he could peddle to the cops if he happens to get arrested for something that has nothing to do with you. Unfortunately, the majority of grow room busts are made because the police were tipped off about them.

Before you ever start growing, you should consider who might find out, how you could prevent them from finding out, and what may happen to you if they actually found out. This includes best friends, girlfriends and boyfriends, relatives, unexpected guests, and even your husband or wife. Relationships can and do go sour for thousands of different reasons and you don't want to give anyone any "revenge ammo" if things go bad.

Maybe a nephew finds something in your basement and tells his teacher. Maybe you cheated on your girlfriend and now she wants revenge. Maybe your parents flip out and try to "save you from yourself" with a little police intervention. These things *do* happen, but if you're smart, they won't happen to you.

The bottom line is that what you are doing is most likely against the law where you live and if you get caught, you can possibly go to jail. No amount of pride is worth going to jail. Nobody in prison will be impressed.

This chapter will give you tips on how to abide by the three security rules of growing marijuana:

1. Do not tell ANYONE about your grow room.
2. Do not leave a trace when you buy seeds or equipment.
3. Do everything you can to secure and conceal your grow room.

Keep a Low Profile

You make a conscious decision on whether to tell someone about your grow, but you also make decisions on how you conduct yourself when you are growing. Even without directly telling someone about your grow room, you may be indirectly telling people by the way you dress, drive, talk, enter your apartment or even just taking out the trash. Remember, just because you're paranoid, doesn't mean people aren't watching you!

Before you even start buying your equipment, think about the other people who live on your street or in your apartment complex. Most of these people have their own lives: mouths to feed, bills to pay, jobs to wake up for. Start by not interfering with these people. Don't block their cars into their driveways, throw late-night parties, let smoke waft into their living rooms, etc.

When you see your neighbors, smile and make reasonable small talk and then you two can go back to your own lives. It sounds simple, but for a lot of people it isn't. Respect people's right to live their lives peaceably and more often than not, they will do the same for you.

When you wear marijuana-related shirts, cords, dreads, and hemp jewelry, you are asking for trouble. You are certainly free to express yourself, but for your own safety and security, you will want to tone down your love of all things hemp.

Buying Equipment Discreetly

Marijuana odor is always the main concern of growers, but many overlook the signals they give off when they buy equipment and transport it into their homes. After you have done all of your research and grow room planning, you need to decide how you will purchase the equipment and get it into your home without anyone taking notice.

How will you pay for it? What kind of car will you drive? How will you talk to the grow shop owner? What time of day will you bring your equipment into the house? In some areas, these concerns might seem like complete overkill, but in small towns or crowded apartment complexes you should have a plan of action before you ever bring any equipment home.

Dress and Act Appropriately

Most people don't have anything to worry about when they visit their a grow shop. Unfortunately, some people really don't know what they should wear, where they should park, or how they should talk to grow store employees. If you're not sure which category you fit into, this section is for you.

Chances are, you have nothing to worry about when you buy equipment. In many areas, the police have much better things to do than to stake out a grow shop. However, in some cases, the same place you shop for your twenty-plant grow is the same place other people are buying equipment for massive indoor and outdoor growing operations. By following the suggestions below, you'll simply blend into the crowd of other shoppers.

Clothes

Almost every grow shop owner knows what people are using their equipment for. In fact, marijuana growers keep the average hobby hydroponics store in business. Despite what both you and the owner know about where the equipment and supplies are headed, you need to respect the fact that he or she is running a respectable business. The first step in doing that is wearing "average" clothes like jeans and a normal t-shirt. Leave the tie-die, baggy cords, marijuana leaf hat, or anything else that might identify you as a smoker/grower at home. In a perfect world, you shouldn't have to change the way you look, but it's simply for your own protection and keeps the grow shop owner happy to serve you.

Car

Similar to how you dress is the car you drive to the shop and where you park it. If you drive a beat up VW bus/bug covered in Dead stickers, you might want to borrow a car. Any car that's rusted out, smells like marijuana, contains marijuana, or isn't registered should not be driven to the grow shop. If that's not possible, consider parking a few blocks from the hydroponics store. The shop owner should be able to bag your purchases and you can safely carry them to the car undetected.

Attitude

Attitude in this case simply means not directly mentioning why you are buying the equipment. You know and they know what you are growing, so be discreet when asking questions. In the rare case that they don't know and ask you what you are growing, say "tomatoes." Tomatoes grow similarly to marijuana and shouldn't arouse any suspicion.

Never mention yields, strains, marijuana enthusiast magazines or anything else that gives the owner a reason to kick you out of their store. Some owners are cool about it and if you slip up, they'll simply point to the sign that says they can't sell equipment to anyone they know will use it for illegal purposes. However, it's best not to test out how cool the grow shop owner is.

Paying for Equipment

One of the smartest ways to cover your tracks is to not make any to begin with. The first step is to buy all of your equipment using cash. It seems like a paranoid thing to do, but paying with cash gives you piece of mind in knowing that you have no credit card bills or bank statements for someone to use against you. The reason you are using cash is to avoid creating a paper trail that links you or your address to your purchases. Keeping that in mind, never provide your real name or address to the grow shop if they happen to ask for it.

Do not use credit cards

Are you short on cash and thinking about maxing out that credit card? Don't even think about using your plastic. If you have a hydroponics store listed on your credit card statement and someone were to access that statement, they could find out everything you bought with your credit card at that store. It's not worth the risk, so save your money and wait until you can truly afford to grow.

Do not shop online

Shopping online is no different than using a credit card at a hydroponics store except you have the added risk of equipment showing up at your doorstep any time during the day. Browsing online is a great way to research the equipment you need and estimate your costs, but don't follow through with an order. If you do, there will be an order with all of your purchases connected to the address where they were sent to. There can definitely be a cost savings when buying just about anything online, but in this case, the security risks far outweigh any amount of money you can save.

Moving Equipment Into Your Home

Even if the grow shop packs your equipment into bags, you should still have bags or, better yet, large boxes ready to put everything into when you get to your car. If you happen to get pulled over, you just have some plain boxes in your car. When you get home, wait until it's dark before moving everything into your house or apartment. It can be hassle, but it keeps suspicion to a minimum and helps you sleep at night.

Protecting Your Grow Room

Don't Use a Burglar Alarm

A burglar alarm might seem like a good idea for protecting your stash, but think about who really answers the call when someone breaks in? The security company and probably local law enforcement are usually permitted to enter your home if an alarm is tripped. These are two groups you do not want poking in and around your home no matter who might be inside. This is especially true when you go on vacation because you might be in for a big surprise when you get home.

If you are truly worried about your safety when living in your home, you shouldn't be growing marijuana there. If you are more interested in keeping people from stealing your belongings, consider a good home owners insurance policy. That way your valuables are covered and you won't get any untimely visits from the police.

Padlock the Room

Padlocking your grow room is a surprisingly effective way of keeping a casual snoop from peeking at your plants. It can also draw suspicion, but with a lock in place, there is no way for them to confirm it. Also, if you are wondering if someone has been into your grow room, you will know for sure if you find a broken padlock on the floor. It certainly won't keep someone determined to get to your plants out, but it should still be an essential part of your grow room security.

Stealth Trash Disposal

You might think that waiting until the moment the trash collector drives down your street is a good time to put your trash out. Unfortunately, you aren't the only one who knows about this technique. One way to confirm a house is used for growing is to watch how the owner deals with his trash. Warrants have been signed for this type of behavior, so it's wise to not to have any of your grow room trash associated with your home.

The best method is to double-bag any incriminating evidence in large black trash bags, put those bags in a cardboard box, and take the box out to your car. Remember not to include anything that can connect you to the contents of the bag. Then, sometime during the course running a few errands, find a discreet trash bin that you can dump the bags into. Don't forget to keep the box for later use.

Odor Control

Odor control is one of, if not *the* biggest, security concerns a grower can have. Unless you live on a farm or some other faraway location and never get any visitors, you will have to figure out what to do with the smells wafting out of your grow room.

Plant odor is something that needs to be considered before you ever start growing, because once the smell gets out, it can be hard to contain. Another problem is that, as a grower living near your crop, you might get used to the smell and think it's not that bad. Unfortunately, your first visitor might tell you otherwise.

By planning ahead on where you will vent your grow room air and/or how to remove the odor from it, *your* nose will be the first to signal whether your methods are effective instead of your neighbors, parents, or the police. By taking your particular circumstances into consideration, such as how close you live to other people, how many plants you are growing, and how often you get visitors, you can decide which of the following options will be effective.

Just remember that whatever you have to pay for odor removal is a fraction of the cost you might have to spend if you get caught growing something illegal.

Ionizers

Air ionizers work by generating negatively charged ions and dispersing them into the air. When these negative ions come in contact with positively charged particles floating in the air, like dust, pollen, or other odorous molecule, they change the particles' positive charge to negative, causing the neutralized particle to fall to the ground. This process results in cleaner air, but also dirtier floors and walls.

Although ionizers are inexpensive and easy to find, many growers are now opting for more effective solutions. For even modest grow rooms, ionizers are often insufficient in completely eliminating marijuana grow room odors. Because they work by causing particles to precipitate, or fall to the ground, they create a lot of dust that has to be cleaned up. Because ionizers don't effectively eliminate odors they are not recommended for anyone growing more than a plant or two.

Ozone Generators

Ozone (O_3) is one of the most powerful ways to eliminate grow room odors. Ozone doesn't mask odors like air fresheners, it neutralizes odors at the source, then harmlessly converts to CO_2 and oxygen. In nature, ozone is generated as a by-product of electrical current in the air and accounts for the wonderful fresh air scent after a lightning storm, and of course the ozone layer is created by the UV radiation of the sun.

Ozone is used by marijuana growers to destroy the tell-tale odors given off by their plants. Commercially, ozone is produced using either ultraviolet light (UV) or corona discharge (CD). CD technology passes air over electrically charged metal plates and produces the highest concentrations of ozone. UV technology passes air over an ultraviolet bulb to achieve the same result at lower concentrations.

CD ozonators, although powerful, have a number of drawbacks compared to their UV counterparts. CD, is more expensive, requires more maintenance and creates a build-up of nitric acid. Nitric acid is highly corrosive to plants, ventilation duct work and to the unit itself. The biggest drawback to CD units is the amount of ozone that it produces. At high concentrations, ozone merely replaces one identifiable odor for another and can be harmful to your health.

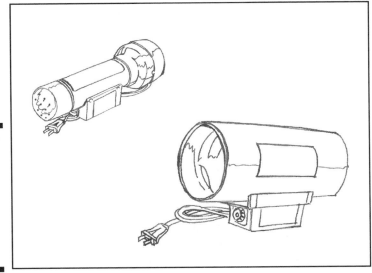

Figure 9-1:
Ozone
generators
are
designed
to connect
into your
exhaust
ducting.

Ultra violet light is the preferred method for ozone air deodorization. UV units are less expensive, require less maintenance and provide an effective level of ozone concentration without identifiable exhaust gasses. All at less energy consumption than a 100 watt light bulb. UV generators are the most popular for indoor growing and are highly recommended over CD generators.

Ozone Safety

There has been some debate over the safety of ozone and humans. However, the EPA, USDA and OSHA have approved the use of ozone at concentrations of 0.1 PPM, for an exposure period of eight hours, without any side effects. Most UV home ozone generators produce less than .05 PPM, and exposure time is minimal. With this in mind, ozone generation is a safe and effective method of odor control.

Placement

Most generators are four, six, or eight-inch diameter tubes, designed to connect directly inline with an air exhaust system. This method is the safest and most effective way to use your ozone generator, but for added advantages, if you divert some ozone back into the grow room it will help kill airborne substances such as spores and molds, which helps keep your grow sterile and clean.

If your generator is pumping ozone directly into your grow room, you will need to have a strong ventilation system to help keep the levels of ozone from building up to dangerous levels. Having the exhaust air vented outdoors is the best solution. Avoid spending excess amounts of time in your grow area if you are using an ozone generator.

Place the ozonator units in the exhaust line or area or within the grow area itself, above an air circulation or intake/exhaust duct or fan. Purchase a timer to run continuously, except for 30 minutes before and during your scheduled maintenance times.

If you must treat the air inside the grow room due to room leaks/smell seepage it is preferable to use a UV ozone generator. UV ozonators using a frequency of 185nm (approx) do not produce nitric acid as a by-product like corona discharge ozonators do. Thus corona discharge ozone generators should only be used in the exhaust system. If using a UV ogzone generator to treat the air inside the room this could damage your plants if the concentration is too high.

Maintenance

A UV bulb gets coated with dust, which reduces the amount of light emitted and therefore the amount of ozone produced. The bulb should be cleaned at least monthly to maintain peak performance. If you have never cleaned your bulb, you are diminishing the unit's effectiveness and will be surprised with the improvement in odor control afterwards.

Activated Carbon Filters

Activated carbon has been in use for centuries as an air/water purifier, health supplement, and chemical "scrubber," in fact activated carbon has some of the strongest physical adsorption properties of any material even known. Activated carbon or charcoal is made by burning hardwood, nutshells, coconut husks, animal cones and/or other carbonaceous materials.

Charcoal becomes activated by heating it with steam to high temperature levels in the absence of oxygen. This removes any non-carbon elements and produces a porous internal microstructure with an extremely high surface area. A single gram of a high quality activated charcoal can have 400-2000 square meters of surface area, 98% of which is internal.

The surface area of activated charcoal is where the unwanted molecules are adsorbed and trapped. Adsorption means the impurities in the air are attached to the surface of the activated carbon by a chemical attraction. When certain chemicals pass next to the carbon surface, they attach to the surface and are trapped.

Activated carbon manufactured from coconut husk has one of the largest activated surface areas combined with a high percentage of micro pores. For this reason activated charcoal manufactured from coconut husk is used in a wide range of air purification systems including indoor gardening. Where indoor air quality is being compromised by odors and gases, air filtration with coconut husk-activated carbon is the safest and most effective way of dealing with the problem.

Figure 9-2: Carbon filters with and without a protective sock.

Since activated charcoal is no more than an amorphous form of carbon - meaning it has no regular atomic structure like the other forms of elemental carbon (diamond, graphite etc), it is completely safe to use and handle.

Placement

Carbon filters are available in different sizes to accommodate the various sizes of grow rooms. They are usually made of steel and manufactured in the shape of a long tube. You can usually choose a filter with a specific sized intake flange such as four, six, or eight inches. You can connect your ducting directly to this flange.

For the stealthiest application, you will want to connect your exhaust fan to your carbon filter using standard duct tubing inside your grow room. Any odor given off by the plants will be sucked into the exhaust fan, sent through the filter, then back into the grow room along with fresh air brought in through the air intake vent.

Since carbon filters can be quite large, many growers place them outside of the grow room, but still out of plain view. The exhaust fan still pushes all of the grow room air through the filter via ducting, but the air doesn't go back directly into the grow room. Growers prefer this option because it ensures that their plants get as much fresh, CO_2-rich air as possible.

Maintenance

Despite the huge adsorption capacity and surface area of coconut based activated carbon, eventually the material will need to be replaced, so always follow the manufactures recommendations on how often this should be carried out so that your growing environment stays clean and fresh smelling.

If you purchased the correct filter size for your grow room, you shouldn't have to replace the carbon more than once every three or four months. You will know for sure when you start smelling marijuana from outside your garden. If this happens, you should immediately replace the carbon.

Concealing your Grow Room

While controlling the odor of your grow room can be costly, concealing your grow room is usually just a matter of planning and attention to detail. The following sections explain a few tips on how keep your grow room from being be seen, heard, or felt.

Light Leaks

If you've ever seen a grow room you already know that they are both hot and bright, a by-product of the HID lights illuminating the plants. Light leaks are particularly problematic when you have guests visiting that may walk near your grow room. The intense light beaming from the cracks of the door can't be explained away easily because it is far brighter than any ordinary lamp.

To check for light leaks you should wait until it's late at night, turn off all of your lights except for the HID lamps, wait for a few minutes for your eyes to adjust and then inspect your grow room from every conceivable angle. You will know a light leak when you see it and it's likely that you will find a few the first time you check.

Solving a light leak is fairly easy and usually requires just a few household items to get the job done. The two most common items used to block light are duct tape and foam weather stripping. If you don't have either, you can pick them up at any hardware store.

With the main lights still off, you can get to work with both the foam and tape to cover any cracks until you can't see any light coming from the room. You should check for leaks for the next few nights until finally you turn off all the lights and the grow room is completely undetectable. You will also want to periodically check for leaks if you expect visitors during the evening.

Venting Hot Air

Depending on where you live, the hot air expelled from the exhaust fans may not be a problem. In fact, if it gets cold in your region the hot air can save you money on your heating bill. For most people, it can become a problem and there are a few of dealing with it.

If you are using an activated charcoal filter or a ozone generator and you determine that the air is safe to vent outside, then you have solved your problem. Some connect their ducting to the same attachment used with a clothes dryer. To be on the safe side, you will still want to protect this vent and make sure no one has direct access to it. This helps prevent people from asking you why you dry your clothes twelve to twenty-four hours a day. Other people vent down the sewer or through a skylight. It all depends on where your grow room is and how close your neighbors are.

Another option is to vent it directly into your living area and use an air conditioner to lower the temperature. This can get expensive, but for some people it is the only safe option.

Fan Noise

It's important to remember that the air moving through the intakes and exhausts make noise, as well as the fan itself. Some of the fan noise from vibration can be overcome by mounting the fan in a non-rigid manner. The fans can me mounted using rubber grommets to help dampen the vibration. Self-adhesive foam rubber window insulation can also be used. In some installations, it can be mounted by threading a bungee cord through each mounting hole, then attaching the other ends of the bungee cord to the exhaust hole.

Generally, air moving through duct work or tubing can become noisy, particularly if the air has to move at a higher velocity. More, larger diameter intakes and vent tubes will generally be quieter than fewer, smaller diameter intakes and vents. The fans also don't have to work quite as hard. Also, although popular and easy to use, flexible "accordion-style" ducting, commonly used to connect clothes dryers to external vents, are not always the best choice as they cause a great deal of drag and make the fans work harder. Generally air flowing through them is noisier than smoother duct work.

Chapter 10

Seeds and Seedlings

· ·

In This Chapter

▶ Exploring different strains and characteristics

▶ Finding out how to order seeds

▶ Understanding how seeds germinate into seedlings

▶ Mastering seed germination and transplanting

· ·

Before you can choose the your seeds, you should understand the differences between seedlings and clones. A seedling is a plant that was sprouted from a seed and is the product of sexual reproduction between a male and a female plant. Approximately one-half of these seeds will turn out to be female and the other half will be male. Each and every one, regardless of its sex, will be genetically different.

A clone was never a seed. A clone starts out as a growing tip of a larger established plant (called a "mother" plant), which was cut off, treated with a rooting hormone and put into its own small container. The growing tip eventually sprouts roots and becomes its own separate plant, genetically identical to the plant that it was taken from. A clone will always be the same sex as its "mother;" with the same growth traits, the same potential potency, and the same flavor and high.

Cloning is considered an advanced technique compared to growing from seed. Unless you have access to high quality clones from another grower, you will have to create clones yourself. This requires additional time, equipment, and a completely different growing arrangement. Because of this, a separate chapter is devoted to clones and mother plants. If you plan to grow for many years, you should consider cloning, otherwise you should probably start with seeds.

Acquiring Seeds

There are over 2000 genetically unique cannabis strains growing throughout the world. Several thousand years ago, there may have been no more than 20-30 native strains, each with its own unique character. Today, the cultivation scene is full of exotically named strains that attempt to indicate the size, aroma, THC content, or other characteristic of the strain.

In order to get the seeds that will work best in your situation, you need to consider what kind of seeds you need and how to get them. The following sections describe how the marijuana seeds are classified and what characteristics you might find listed with a particular strain. You will also learn where to get seeds, how to pay for them, and where you should send them.

Varieties of Marijuana

It can sometimes be overwhelming when trying to decide which seeds you should get and how to acquire them. Picking which variety is not as difficult as you may think. There are really only two major sides of the marijuana family: Indicas and Sativas.

Indicas

Indicas originally came from the hash producing countries of the world like Afghanistan, Morocco, and Tibet. They are short dense plants, with broad leaves and often grow a darker green. After flowering starts, they mature in six to eight weeks. The buds will be thick and dense, with flavors and aromas ranging from pungent skunk to sweet and fruity. The smoke from an Indica is generally a body-type stone, relaxing and laid back.

Sativas

Sativas are tall, thin plants, with much narrower leaves and grow a lighter green in color. They grow very quickly and can reach heights of 20 feet in a single outdoor season. They originally come from Colombia, Mexico, Thailand and Southeast Asia. Once flowering has begun, they can take anywhere from ten to sixteen weeks to fully mature. Flavors range from earthy to sweet and fruity. The stone of a Sativa is cerebral, up and energetic.

Hybrids

Hybrid strains are the result of combining (breeding) different indicas, different sativas or a combination of both types. The resulting hybrid strains will grow, mature and smoke in relationship to the indica/sativa percentages they contain. The actual percentages of indica and sativa that a strain contains are almost impossible to calculate precisely and not all breeders provide this information.

Strain Characteristics

Indicas and hybrids are the recommended varieties to grow indoors. Beyond which variety is the right one for your situation, each individual strain has its own set of characteristics that further determine which ones will work best for you.

The following are some of the types of information that seeds banks include in their strain listings. Use this information as a guideline for finding the types of marijuana that will flourish in your growing environment and provide the type of high you are looking for.

Outdoor or indoor

Assuming that you are growing indoors, don't choose strains that are listed for outdoor growing. Genetically speaking, their growing characteristics don't always transfer very well to growing indoors. Outdoor strains can be conditioned to grow indoors, but it may take a few crops to settle them into a vastly different growing environment. Flowering times and yields listed by seed distributors are approximate and can vary depending on conditions.

Height

If height is listed for an indoor/outdoor strain, it is usually referring to the average size of the plant when it is grown to full size. When growing indoors, you have great control over how tall your plants get by the amount of time you grow them in the vegetative phase before initiating flowering. Artificial lights do not efficiently penetrate much more than three feet down into a garden, so it makes little sense to grow them any larger than that.

After the light schedule is changed to twelve hours on and twelve hours off, flowering will begin in about seven to fourteen days. During this time, the plants will continue to grow another six to fourteen inches. How much they will grow depends on the indica/sativa ratio of the strain. Sativas will stretch the most. Depending on this ratio, flowering should be initiated at around eighteen to 24 inches to achieve an end height of 36 inches. How long it will take to get this tall depends on the strain and the conditions in the garden.

Price and quality

You may find some strains with identical names in various seed company catalogues and web sites that have enormously different prices. First determine that the seed company is reputable by doing a search on the internet or by reading message boards. You can also find web sites that rate most of the popular seed distributors and may include comments from other cultivators that describe their experience with the company and their product. Considering the price of seeds and the multitude of bogus seed banks, this research should not be considered optional.

If the company is on the up and up, the typical reason for such a disparity in price is that the more expensive strains are coming from the major seed banks in Amsterdam. These seed banks have spent over 20 years inventing and developing their strains, many of which have been multiple competition winners and are considered some of the best in the world and as a result command a higher price in the marketplace.

The lesser-priced strains of the same name come from breeders who have taken those Dutch genetics, grown them themselves, have chosen the parents carefully and produced seeds. They didn't invent the strain and haven't done the same amount of work to command the same high prices. The quality is usually the same, but the plants may be somewhat different from the originals, depending on the parents chosen.

Potency

The majority of strains found at reputable seed distributors are considered potent. The success of the eventual outcome depends on your personal tastes and the conditions in which they are grown. A mediocre seed grown in the best environment can produce very potent buds. Conversely, a cup-winning strain grown under weak lighting and improper curing can produce buds with a weak high.

THC percentages listed for a strain are dubious because the results cannot be independently verified. The percentage is supposedly indicative of the strength of the "high" that strain can achieve when ingested, but no matter how much resin you induce on an indica, it's still not going to give you the stone of a sativa.

The potency of any strain has more to do with your own personal tastes and expectations than a percentage. For the most part, don't concern yourself with the potency listed for a particular strain, most will produce mind-blowing highs when grown properly.

Yield

Any yield or harvest amount listed for the strains are approximate and depend a lot on how they are grown and the quality of the environment. Indoor lights don't penetrate down very far, so it's better to grow a larger number of smaller plants to achieve the highest yield of top quality bud. Maximum yields indoors are achieved with indicas and mostly indica hybrids, while the more sativa in the mix, the lower the yields tend to be.

Indoor yield is really limited by the amount of light available to the plants, not the strain you choose. If you've designed a good a good growing environment, you can expect the yield to be about the same from any strain in relationship to its indica/sativa ratio. It is up to you to maximize your plants' potential in your grow space. To do this, you may need to experiment with different strains to find which will respond best in your environment.

Flowering times

Flowering times listed for strains in catalogues and web sites are an indication of how long it takes the plant to mature indoors after flowering has be induced. The length of the flowering phase can be influenced by the environment to some degree, but is mostly determined by strain genetics and the individual plant itself. Indicas flower faster than sativas and hybrids flowering times are in relationship to the percentage of sativa/indica they contain. The more sativa in the hybrid strain, the longer it will take to flower.

Equally important to your overall harvest is vegetation time, or how long you grow them before flowering is induced. Sativas grow quickly and if you wait too long to flower them, they will outgrow the limits of the space. On the other hand, if an indica is not grown for long enough, the yield can be greatly reduced.

Ten Great Strains to Get You Started

If you're not sure which strains you want or if you're just overwhelmed by the selection, the following list of strains are all suitable for indoor growing and are available through many seed banks. The strains are listed in no particular order, but they're all champions in the potency department.

Northern Lights

Northern Lights is highly adapted to indoor growing. Nearly all promising modern indoor strains contain NL genes. High flower-to-leaf ratio, compact buds, good yields and exceptional resin production are all characteristics displayed by this wonderful plant. The smoke is full bodied yet somewhat neutral in flavor.

Flowering time: 7-8 weeks

White Widow

In the mid-1990's a legend was born. White Widow almost instantly appeared on about every coffee shop menu in Holland. This masterpiece has set the standard for the "White" strains. White Widow grows tall with delicate arms. Buds are moderately compact in order to contain the copious amounts of resin. Leaning on the sativa side, the buzz is powerful yet energetic and very social.

Flowering time: 8-9 weeks

Big Bud

This is a good plant for professional cash croppers who don't want to compromise in quality. Even experienced growers continue to be amazed and come back to fill their garden with these heavy ladies. It is advisable to tie up the bottom branches as they have a tendency to break due to their excessive weight. Big Bud has some Skunk characteristics and a fairly long lasting high.

Flowering time: 8-9 weeks

AK-47

An easy-growing good producer, this strain's power earned it the name. "AK" has won multiple awards at the "Cup" over the years. These plants produce hard, compact buds that gleam with resin crystals and have a full rich flavor. AK-47 is considered to be one of the strongest early finishing strains available.

Flowering time: 7-8 weeks

Super Skunk

Super Skunk is a successful attempt to beef up the famous Skunk #1. This strain is one of the first to match the potency of the powerful import hashish in coffee shops. Still famous for its potent flavor and strong high. Much easier to grow and manicure than the "white" strains. Yields can be very financially interesting. Also works well in greenhouse or shed operations.

Flowering time: 7-8 weeks

Blueberry

Blueberry is a mostly Indica strain, that dates to the late 1970's. A large producer under optimum conditions, this dense and stout plant with red, purple and finally blue hues, usually cures to lavender blue. The finished product has a very fruity aroma and taste of blueberry. It produces a notable and pleasantly euphoric high of the highest quality and is very long lasting. Blueberry has a long shelf life and stores well over a long period.

Flowering time: 7-8 weeks

Bubble Gum

Bubble Gum was developed by growers in Indiana, USA. From there the genetics moved to New England and eventually Holland. Here the decision was made to bring the several different phenotypes, all named Bubble Gum, down to one type of plant. It took many generations to finally produce a stable Bubble Gum strain that had a sweet smell and euphoric high; the original trademarks of this famous strain. The result is a short broad-leafed plant which grows a compact heavy bud with a very white, crystalline appearance.

Flowering time: 7-8 weeks

Master Kush

Originally known as High-rise, this Hindu Kush/Skunk hybrid was stabilized and marketed as Master Kush. It has been a classic ever since. A strong plant of medium height and bushiness, Master Kush is a heavy producer with in hydroponic grow rooms. The earthy smell of Master Kush is strong and the smoke is smooth.

Flowering time: 6-7 weeks

Afghani #1

Originally this strain was imported from Afghanistan and selectively bred in Holland for indoor cultivation. Afghan has a strong acrid aroma. Greasy resin glands extend to the fat shade leaves. The smoke is heavy with a strong almost numbing buzz if raised and cured properly. This plant has a high flower to leaf ratio and good yield. Afghan is one of the original genetic lines used in many popular modern day hybrids.

Flowering time: 7-9 weeks

Silver Haze

Although the cerebral high of the Sativa is preferred by many, indoor growers aren't too fond of them because they grow too tall and have lower yields than Indicas. Through a lot of cross breeding, a superb Indica/Sativa hybrid suited for indoor growing was developed. The breeders managed to get the height and flowering time of the plant down to an acceptable level and still retain the unique Sativa qualities of the high. The yields from this strain are lower than traditional Indicas, but the difference in high makes it worthy to grow indoors.

Flowering time: 9-10 weeks

Using Bag or Found Seeds

It's generally thought that bag seeds are unreliable for producing great marijuana. The main argument is that you don't know exactly what you are growing and it may be the wrong type of strain to grow in your environment. On the other hand, if the bag was great smoke and you don't have access to clones or don't want to risk ordering seeds, bag seeds may be your only option. At the very least, make sure your seeds are viable for growing.

Fresh seeds have a waxy glimmer and a hard, intact shell. Colors range from a buff through a dark brown, and from light grey to almost black colors. Often seeds are mottled with brown or black spots, or lines on a lighter field.

Green or whitish seeds are usually immature and will germinate feebly if at all. Shiny, very dark brown or black seeds often mean the contents are fermented and the embryo is dead. Fermented seeds crush easily with finger pressure and are hollow or dusty inside. Brick or compressed cannabis seeds must be checked, as seeds that are bruised or crushed are not viable.

Choosing a Reputable Seed Bank

In the past, distribution of cannabis seeds were limited to the local geographic region of the breeders and growers. Over the years, seed banks have become more advanced with worldwide distribution of a larger variety of cannabis seeds than ever before. The supply of seed stock originates from single individual breeders to large breeding greenhouses throughout the world. A seed bank is an institution, which stores and supplies consumers with diverse varieties of cannabis seeds, both domestically and abroad.

When selecting a seed bank, you should read the various charts and ratings as well as ask others what seed banks they recommend. Once you've narrowed down your choices, you should visit and/or e-mail the seed banks to learn more about them, their products, and how they conduct business.

Keep in mind that the majority of seed banks will send product as promised and often the decision of what seed bank to order from will come down to product availability, price, speed, and the desired payment method.

When should I order my seeds?
It can take weeks, sometimes more than a month, for your seed order to finally show up at your door. Consider ordering your seeds before you ever start buying equipment. If you have problems with your order, you will still have time to re-order before you find yourself staring at a grow room, all set up and no place to grow.

Ordering Seeds

Lately, the number of seed banks appearing online has exploded, which means you need to be extra careful who you order from and how you pay. Some seed banks have been in business for ten years or longer and have a great reputation for reliable orders and fast shipment. They also charge a premium price which may cause you to look at some of the newer seed banks sprouting up. Before you order form any of these companies, do your research and see if they even have a reputation and whether it's a good one.

The ordering process at many seed banks is as simple as filling out a form and pressing a button. Often an e-mail confirmation is sent back and then the customer sends payment. And assuming no problems, the seed packets are eventually received. Be sure to include any applicable surcharges in your payment and follow all ordering instructions carefully.

Money order

Using a money order is absolutely the best way to pay for your seeds. They are untraceable and most seed banks prefer this method of payment. If you are sending a money order, be sure you send the correct type (most require international money orders) and in the correct currency amount. If you're unsure, ask the seed bank before sending anything. Take similar precautions when mailing, just as you would with cash.

Cash

If you have to send cash, send a few large bills instead of many smaller ones. Many bills can cause the envelope to bulge, be over-weight, or even be detected by drug sniffing dogs since most paper money contains drug residue. Bills should be tightly enclosed in paper, a card, etc., to hide their contents so it isn't visible when the envelope is viewed under bright light.

Also, be sure to seal the envelope well, but not too well. The trick is that it's secure and yet can be easily examined without raising suspicion. Typically, mail is opened at a corner when examined. If you can open a small hole in a corner of the envelope and all you see is paper that looks like a normal letter and see no bills, then it is packed well and will most likely make it to its destination. Just remember, there is always a chance of interception, even with the best of methods.

Credit card

If you pay by credit card, be sure to pay using a secure order form. You can confirm that you're using a secure form by clicking on Security or similar in your web browser while you are ordering. Be aware that credit card payments will leave a paper trail and may be illegal from where you are as well as technically illegal for the seed bank. Unless you are sure of all the risks and consequences, avoid the credit card payment method.

Western Union

If you pay by Western Union, or a bank transfer, be sure you know exactly how the seed company wants you to do it. If you have any doubts, e-mail the seed bank or consider paying another way. As with a credit card, this method can open you up to security risks that can easily be avoided. If, for whatever reason you must wire the money, follow the seed bank instructions precisely, as they know the safest way to make the transfer

Seed Bank Problems

Various seed bank problems include late delivery, partial delivery, no delivery, or delivery of inferior product. In most instances you are at the mercy of the seed bank and it's usually best to discuss problems via e-mail.

If all else fails, e-mail the seed bank supplier of the strain(s) you ordered. Some seed suppliers will back up their products if the seed bank fails to do so and/or terminate their relationship with that particular seed bank. Ultimately the seed bank business, due to its very nature, is dependent on trust of both buyer and seller. Most orders are completed without incident every day.

Seed Legalities

Cannabis seeds contain absolutely no cannabinoids (THC) and thus are legal (or at least tolerated) in many countries throughout the world. But in the United States, cannabis seeds are illegal to possess or import or export. However, seeds *may* be legal if traded within a state such as California, if intended for personal medical use.

Realistically, the risks involved with purchasing/trading seeds is quite small to the buyer. Often the worst that happens is that the seeds are intercepted and you receive a letter from the customs department explaining that illegal contraband was found in mail addressed to you and that you may contest it, which you should never do. Always have seeds sent through regular first class mail to an address other than the grow location to minimize legal risks.

Seed Storage

Keep your seeds at room temperature in small, airtight containers with a desiccant or silica gel pack (found in new shoes and clothing pockets) that is never in direct contact with the seeds. Put those containers into a larger one and store it in a cool, dry place.

Keep the seed containers in the attic in the winter and move them to the coolest, moisture-free part of the house in the summer. For storage of more than two years, you might consider freezing them. The trick is to keep the temperature steady and defrost them on a cool, dry day. If you have a crappy freezer, you might ruin some seeds.

Long Term Storage

For uninterrupted long-term storage, freezing in a vacuum pack with a desiccant is best. Each time a batch of seeds goes through a freeze/thaw cycle, a few become unusable. For storage lengths of a few years or less, room temperature storage in an airtight container with a desiccant is satisfactory. Vacuum packing with desiccant and room temperature storage is best for access without having to thaw and re-freeze them.

The problem with using a refrigerator for any period of time is the excessive amount of moisture that is constantly present. Each time the door is opened, moisture condenses on items inside, for which the desiccant is an inadequate deterrent for molds. A vacuum-sealed container should not condense moisture on the inside and is recommended when using a refrigerator or any other long term storage. Seeds can be viable even after sitting around for ten years if they are properly stored.

Germination

Now that you've got your seeds, it's time to germinate them. Germination is the stage when your plant shows its first signs of life. There are numerous methods on how to germinate your seeds. The procedure below seems to be the most commonly used and is certainly easy to do. Just follow the steps and you should germinate most, if not all, of your precious seeds.

Easy Germination

You can easily germinate your seeds using a paper towel. With this method, water is supplied through a damp paper towel and is absorbed through a small hole on the blunt end of your seeds. Once they have soaked up enough water, they will crack open and root tips begin to emerge. During the process of germination you must make sure the towel never dries out or the partially germinated seeds will also dry out and never sprout.

There are different methods that prove successful. Seeds can be placed between folded, wet paper towels that are kept moist and warm in an area between 70-85°, such as on the top of the refrigerator. After a period of 48 hours to a week, the vast majority of viable seeds will crack open with a white root tip emerging. At this point, the seed is gently placed in the growing medium approximately ½ inch deep with the root tip pointed downward.

Direct Germination

Seeds can also be placed directly into the grow medium with the pointed end facing upwards to germinate without having to transplant them later on. The medium is kept uniformly moist until the young seedling emerges on the surface.

It is not necessary to provide light before the seedlings break the surface, but it is beneficial to have strong light present from that moment forward to prevent excessive stem elongation. Fluorescent lighting is satisfactory with cool white or higher color temperature tubes being preferable. Metal halide lighting is beneficial, if heat and moisture are monitored.

Figure 10-1:
Fold the seeds into the paper towel and keep moist, not wet.

How do seeds start growing?
A seed begins it's germination process by absorbing water. Water swells the seed coat and brings the dormant plant inside the seed back to life. Following that, the seed coat cracks and the ratticle emerges from the seed, and forms into the root. The hypocotyl elongates, pushing two cotyledons above the surface. As the cotyledons are pushed above ground, the seed coat usually falls off. The plant then uses up the energy stored in the endosperm (which is the middle part of the cotyledons) and begins producing leaves. Once the true leaves are produced, the plant photosynthesizes to produce its own food.

Transplanting

If you've chosen the paper towel/plastic bag method of germination, you can either transplant the germinated seeds directly into your hydroponics system or you can transplant them into an intermediate growing area that will ensure that you get the healthiest seedlings possible. Unless you are already experienced with your growing equipment, transplanting into a grow tray with a humidity dome and heating pad is your best option.

The secondary stage in the life of the plant is the most delicate one and requires the most attention to your plants' health. If you've already invested time, money, and risk in getting good seeds, it's worth the extra expense to "baby" them from sprout to vigorous seedling. Plus, if you decide you want to start cloning, you can use all of the following equipment in the future.

Equipment

If you decide to transplant your germinated seeds into an intermediate growing area, you will need the following equipment:

Heating pad

You can help the seedling process by using a heat pad. By purchasing a heat pad designed specifically for gardening, your temperature should be set correctly. However, if you buy a commercial heat pad, make sure to keep the temperature setting on low.

The water in your propagation tray should never reach 80°F (70-75°F is best). If the average temperature in your growing area is already within these limits, you probably don't need a heating pad.

One-inch rockwool or starter cubes

Starter cubes are used to hold your germinated seedling upright and to give it just enough medium to enable root growth. Starter cubes can be bought individually, but you may want to consider buying a "sheet" of these cubes to make them easier to work with in the seedling tray.

Seedling tray

Seedling trays hold the starter cubes in place and can accommodate a humidity dome if you choose to buy one. You could also use a substitute such as a baking sheet or any shallow plastic container instead of a traditional seedling tray. Whether you choose a tray or a substitute, make sure that neither has holes on the bottom because you need the tray to hold a small amount of water for the roots to access.

Humidity dome

After the seeds have germinated, you may want to put a humidity dome on the propagation tray, over the seedlings, for the first week or two. Humidity domes are made of hard, clear plastic and fit over top of all the plants. Make sure it has at least four 1" diameter air holes drilled into it. It is not absolutely necessary to use a humidity dome but it will lead to very healthy plant growth.

Lighting

After your root tips sprout from your seeds, they will need some light. The light should be on for at least eighteen hours per day. Many growers choose to apply the standard 18/6 lighting regimen, at least during the seedling stage. This lighting regiment induces solid initial growth in the plants.

Although there are many types of lighting that you can use for your seedlings, many growers use fluorescent (cool white/blue spectrum) lighting or sun-grow spectrum combination lights (blue and red spectrum) when germinating seedlings. This form of lighting offers a broad spectrum like the sun and usually come in a four foot fixture. Most types of lighting will not hurt your plants or seedlings, but fluorescent lighting will be the most efficient at this stage.

If you plan to use a HID lamp instead of fluorescent lighting, make sure the light isn't too close the seedlings or it will burn them and/or melt the humidity dome. Check your little seedlings ever hour for the first few hours to make sure they are adjusting to their new environment. If the tops begin to burn raise the light up a few inches and if the seedlings look week and begin to wilt, you need to use a humidity dome.

Nutrients

At this stage you really want to baby your seedlings by watering them gently and not handling them. You should water the plants whenever the medium feels dry to the touch. Mixes composed of Perlite, Vermiculite, and Rockwool and other inert media should be treated with a mild application (300-400 ppm) of fertilizer prior to seedling introduction. You should also check and adjust the pH to 5.5 – 6.2 in order for your plants to access all of the available nutrients. Adding Hormex, Superthrive or some other auxin/vitamin-based supplement will accelerate early plant development.

Step-by-Step Transplanting

Use the following steps to take your germinated seeds and transplant them into an intermediate growing area. If you plan to transplant directly into your hydroponics system, you can skip to Step 4.

Step 1: Mix the nutrient solution

Take out your propagation tray (if you don't have a tray available, you can use a cookie sheet, baking tray, etc.). Fill the tray with water until you have about a ½-inch or 1-inch of water in the bottom. At this point, you can add nutrients or root stimulants of your choice to help the seedlings root more quickly.

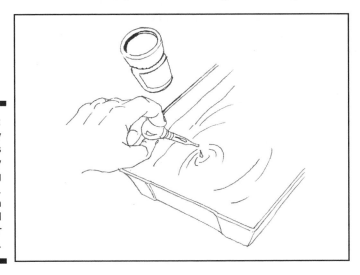

Figure 10-2:
Follow directions carefully when adding nutrients. Too much can be lethal to tender seedlings.

Step 2: Apply solution to the rooting cubes

After you have mixed the water well, you can start cutting up your Rockwool or Oasis cubes. Rinse the them in clean, fresh water before placing them in the propagation tray. Start by tumbling them in the propagation tray of water one by one, until they have absorbed enough water.

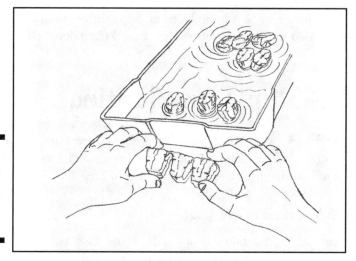

Figure 10-3:
Cubes don't need to be soaked, but uniformly damp.

Step 3: Place germinated seeds into rooting cubes

Now you can start dropping your seeds in the pre-made holes in your starter cubes. Drop the seed in the hole and push a little of the Rockwool or Oasis cube over the hole so your seedlings do not get exposed to light. After you have done that, line them up neatly in the tray and put them under the recommended lighting.

Germinated seeds usually take one to two weeks to become full grown seedlings. You should also refresh your water to compensate for evaporation. Each time you change the water also remember to gradually add more nutrient and rooting solution to you propagation tray. This will keep your seedlings and baby plants very healthy.

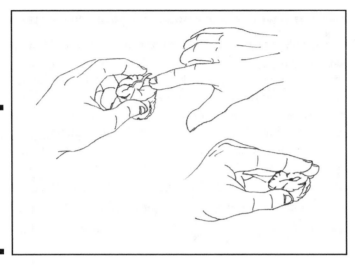

Figure 10-4:
Germinated
seeds
are very
sensitive.
Use a fold
from the
rockwool to
protect them.

Once your seedlings reach two inches tall, bend their stems back and forth to force it to be very thick and strong. Spindly stems cannot support heavy flowering growth. After transplanting your seedlings, an internal oscillating fan will reduce your humidity on the leave's stomata and improve the stem strength as well.

Figure 10-5:
Rockwool
cubes
shouldn't be
submerged
in water.

Step 4: Transplant seedlings to your hydroponics system

When your plants have reached two to three inches and have plenty of white healthy roots, they should be ready to transplant to your hydroponics system. Start by setting your rockwool or oasis cubes in the bottom of your larger pots with the baby plant sticking straight up. Lightly apply grow rocks, loose Rockwool, or any other medium you have decided on, around the Rockwool or Oasis cube until it is completely covered and the pot is full. If possible, add some vitamin B-1 or transplant nutrient to your reservoir take to insure that your baby plants will survive the transplant.

Figure 10-6:
Don't "pack" the rockwool cube, allow for air to reach the tender roots.

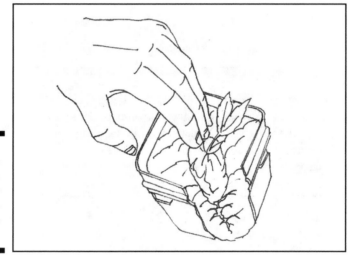

Chapter 11

Vegetative Growth

· ·

In This Chapter

▶ Lighting and feeding during the vegetative phase

▶ Pruning and training your plants

▶ Identifying male, female and hermaphrodite plants

▶ When to initiate the flowering phase

· ·

Vegetative growth is the second major phase in the life of a plant after it completes germination and begins photosynthesis. During this stage a plant will grow as large as it can before the onset of the flowering phase. Essentially, it is the period of growth between germination and the beginning of sexual maturity characterized by flowering.

As the plant starts its vegetative growth, it will photosynthesize as much as possible to grow tall and grow many tips at each pair of leaves. Grow tips are the part of the plant that eventually turn into bud sites. In most indoors grows, the goal is to increase the number of bud sites by pruning and topping the plants as they grow.

Plants can be grown in the vegetative phase indefinitely indoors; it is up to the gardener to decide when to force the plant to flower. A plant can grow from twelve inches to twelve feet before being forced to flower, so there is a lot of latitude for each gardener to manage their garden based on their goals and available space.

While you wait for your plants to grow to twelve inches, twelve feet, or somewhere in-between, you will want to understand how to train and take care of them until you decide to switch your plants to the all-important flowering phase. The following chapter explains the proper lighting and nutrient requirements for plants in the vegetative phase. You will also learn how to train and top your plants so they can use the light they receive most effectively. Finally, you will find out how to tell whether your plant is a male or a female before you begin flowering. With this knowledge, you can remove male plants and ensure a crop of sinsemilla (seedless) plants, if that is what your goal is.

Nutrients

During the vegetative phase you want your plants to receive more nitrogen than phosphorus or potassium. Nitrogen will help your plants grow greener and healthier leaves. If you are using a nutrient line that consists of two or three different stages such as A, B, and C or Grow and Bloom, then your nutrients are pre-balanced. Your Grow or "A" nutrient line will consist of more nitrogen than potassium or phosphorus because nitrogen is the key element for the growth or vegetative phase.

Always read your nutrient labels and make sure you are using the correct amounts for your plant's phase of growth. For vegetative growth, your nutrient's strength level should be between 800-1,200 parts per million (PPM). You can use a metering device to determine the PPM level of your nutrient reservoir as discussed in the Water and Nutrients chapter.

If you aren't using a multi-part nutrient solution designed for hydroponics systems, then you will need to use a generic fertilizer with an N-P-K (Nitrogen-Phosphorus-Potassium) value of 20-20-20. Generic fertilizers aren't generally recommended for growing marijuana, but if that's all you have access to or can afford, then it's better than nothing at all.

Fertilizing should not be done until your plants have reached a height of six inches. Up until a height of six inches, they can survive on water alone. When fertilizing for the first time, you want to mix the strength to ¼ and gradually increase the dosage every few days until it is at full strength.

It is important to watch your plants daily progression; this will help you understand how much water and nutrient your plant is consuming and how fast it is growing. Over-fertilizing is one of the most common mistakes when growing your own marijuana. When your plants are being over-fertilized, the leaf tips will begin to brown. This is commonly known as "fertilizer burn" because the tips appear to be burnt.

Feeding Regiment

Your plants need water and nutrients applied to their root systems every few hours in order to take advantage of the intense light they are receiving. If you apply water constantly or too often, the roots "drown" in the water and the nutrients become toxic to the plants. If you apply water infrequently, the root systems dry up, growth slows, and your plants die.

Most growers divide the irrigation of the plants into six periods during an eighteen-hour light cycle. The first feeding takes place when the lights are switched on. A feeding session follows every three hours until three hours before the lights go off again (the plants should take in nutrients only when the lights are on). If you are using a 24/0 lighting cycle, add two more feedings for a total of eight each day.

In the beginning, don't let the irrigation periods last more than a few minutes, because problems with root development can occur. As your plants stabilize to their nutrient solution and feeding schedule, you can increase the length of the feeding period from a few minutes up to fifteen minutes as the plant grows. Just make sure to carefully watch your plants for the first few days to make sure they aren't being over-saturated in water and nutrients. If this is the case, cut back to a few minutes per feeding until your plants grow larger.

Lighting

As discussed in the Lighting chapter, each phase of plant growth needs a different spectrum of light for plants to grow to their maximum potential. When growing your plants during the vegetative stage, Metal Halide lighting is the recommended bulb type. However, many growers successfully use florescent and High Pressure Sodium bulbs during this phase. For complete information on all of your lighting options, review the Lighting chapter.

Beyond what type of bulb to use, the other important consideration is how much light to provide to your plants each day.

Day Lengths

Although nature provides most areas with some amount of dark period during the night, it is possible to grow your plants vegetatively with no dark period at all. This can increase the speed at which your plants grow by 15-30%. So when you begin growing your seedlings in the vegetative stage, you must decide whether you want to use an 18/6 or 24/0 light cycle.

18/6 refers to the amount of light and dark that the plant receives (eighteen hours of light and six hours of darkness). Providing any more than fourteen hours of light per day will keep the plant in the vegetative phase — growing leaves and not buds. When you want to switch to flowering, you will reduce the cycle to 12/12 (twelve hours of light and twelve hours of darkness).

Can I leave the lights on all the time?
Cannabis plants grow without hassle under twenty-four hours of continuous light. There has been no controlled recordings of increased hermaphrodites or other problems, so most growers now use the full 24/0 cycle.

18/6 does have an advantage in that it allows the equipment and room to cool down. Those six hours of darkness can be timed to happen during the hottest part of the day, providing some relief for growers in hot climates.

Pruning

Pruning is the overall term used for clipping the branches of your plant in order to increase the number of nodes. As a plant begins to flower, nodes become bud sites, so increasing your nodes is a way of increasing the amount of bud your plant can potentially produce. "Topping" is also a form of increasing bud sites, but differs slightly than simple pruning and is covered in the next section.

A **node** is any place on the branches or stem where a leaf attaches and where a new branch begins to grow. Each leaf has its own node. In most cases, the cannabis plant has two opposing leaves and the place they come together at the branch or stem is commonly called a node. However sometimes, as it matures or when the plant is a clone, the formation of leaves is staggered. In this case, each leaf forms its own node.

Pruning is accomplished by using clippers to cut a branch at a 45° angle above an existing node. For every branch that you clip, two new branches will grow from the nearest node and from those branches, more nodes develop. Plants naturally branch out and increase their own node sites, but through pruning, you give mother nature a boost by helping your plants to branch out more frequently.

It is always better to plan a pruning strategy for your developing plants rather than haphazardly clipping off growing tips on an irregular basis. Many growers prune the growing tips after two to four weeks of growth to develop the lower branches, which keeps the plants short and bushy. Pruning should only be done during the vegetative phase unless you have leaves that are dying; you should always cut dying leaves off.

How does pruning affect the size of my plants?

Pruning creates more branches or growing tips, which eventually become more bud sites when the plant is flowering. Effective pruning also helps control the upward and/or outward growth of your plants by keeping them short and bushy.

Pruning Tips

Plan to prune your growing tips in the morning, rather than in the evening, as it gives the plant a full day to recover and heal the wounds. You will want to use a pair of small scissors or a razor blade to prune your plants rather than plucking off the growing tips by hand.

Each time a growing tip is removed, the plant takes a few days to recover before new growth resumes on that branch. It is not recommended that you prune every new node in a developing plant. Rather prune every second or third node to allow the plant time to recover.

Pruning the tallest branches ensures that the lower branches grow upwards, forming a larger surface area for the light to cover. Furthermore, prune your tallest plants first in order to create an even canopy so that one plant doesn't outgrow the others and block their light by creating a shadow.

Over-pruning

Over-pruning can dramatically stunt the growth of your plant. Obviously the bigger your plants are the more they can tolerate a larger portion being chopped. When your plants are small, it's better to err on the side of underpruning so you don't end up with weak, underdeveloped plants.

WEED WARNING

Topping

The overall goal of pruning indoor plants is to increase the number of bud sites, also known as growing tips. The greatest potency of the plant is found in the growing tips. When the plant flowers, these grow tips will produce the dense, potent buds that you've been seeking since you picked up this book. The most effective method of increasing the number of bud sites in a modest-sized indoor grow is by "topping" your plants one or more times.

Topping is a form of pruning where only the very tip of the plant is pinched or clipped off. This will force new branches to develop at the remaining nodes on the branch. Essentially, topping gives you more bud sites near the top of your plant. All of these bud sites will have access to direct light and therefore produce superior budding than shaded, lower-level bud sites. Instead of one large bud at the top of an "untopped" plant, you will get multiple dense buds and ultimately a bigger and better yield.

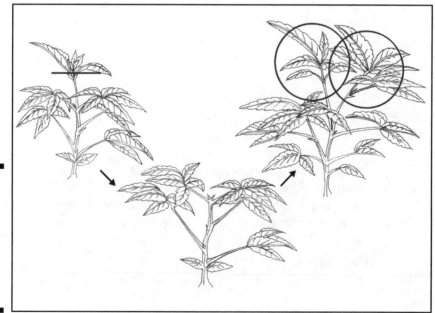

Figure 11-1:
Growth hormones are pushed to the nearby nodes, creating two new "tops."

Topping also helps control the size and shape of the plant as it develops by slowing vertical growth and bushing the plant out. Topping is very beneficial for the indoor grower because it keeps an even garden profile and maximizes the efficiency of the lighting. The intensity of your lighting diminishes with distance from the source. Taller plants do not get intense light near the bottom. Short bushy plants receive light more evenly.

Topping is also done to produce many branches and budding sites. Big cola buds are nice, but it takes large, well-developed stems and branches to hold them up. Smaller branches will have a higher bud-to-stem ratio, allowing the plant to devote more of its resources to flowering than to building and maintaining infrastructure.

WEED WARNING

As with any gardening technique that manipulates a plant's development, you don't want to go crazy with it. Constant topping will slow growth dramatically. Allow the topped plant to grow two nodes for each new top, before repeating the technique.

Thinning

Most marijuana plants need to be "thinned" at some point to encourage the plant to produce as much as possible and remain healthy. Removing lower limbs creates more airflow under the plants in an indoor grow and creates cuttings for cloning. Thinning also forces the plant to focus its growth effort to the top limbs that get the most light, maximizing yields.

If you think that your plant has too much foliage, then you can start by cutting the bottom set of leaves first and work your way up to the top, cutting less as you get higher on the plant. As you work your way up, you want to cut the leaves that are the biggest or leaves that are hanging over the side of the plant. This will help them regenerate new leaves and promote new growth.

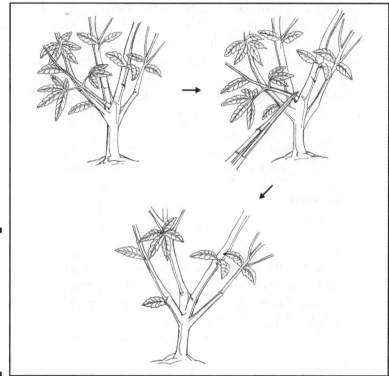

If your plants appear to be healthy and growing the way you want then to, only remove leaves to thin a dense canopy that might shade lower portions of the plant. Try tucking large fan leaves away from offensive areas rather than removing them. While they are out of the way, they will still be soaking up energy for the plant. When they rise up again tomorrow, just tuck them under again. Sound silly? Well, it's worth all the effort you've got.

Although it is recommended that you remove all dying leaves from the plant, you should resist the temptation to prune too many healthy leaves. By severely pruning your marijuana plants you are lowering their resistance to harmful natural enemies such as insects and fungus.

Training

Training is commonly used as part of the Screen of Green technique where you bend the main stem at an angle along a screen to allow the nodes along the bent area to act as tops. A similar form of training can be down without the screen if you find that one or more plants are growing taller than the rest or you simply want to increase the amount of plant surface area exposed to the light.

To "train" your plant, all you need is some string, fishing line, or a roll of bendible twist ties. You start by attaching the string about ¾ up from the bottom of the plant and then pulling that string downward to aim the top of the plant slightly towards the wall. Then, attach the other end of the string to the hydroponics system so that the branch is secure and still slightly bent. Every day or two you can untie the string from the hydroponics system and pull the branch down even further and re-tie the string. After a week or two, the top of your plant will be aimed directly towards the wall at a 90° angle.

Figure 11-3: Tying down a plant exposes the length of the plant to more intense lighting.

Eventually, all of the nodes along the bent portion of the branch will start growing upward towards the light. Even the top that was facing the wall will return to an upright position. Now, more of your plant's surface area will be getting intense HID light instead of just the top. When your plants flower, all of these nodes will produce large cola buds, like a lot of little tops.

WEED WARNING Be very careful when bending the stems of your plants. If you stress the stem too much, it could snap, which would unintentionally "top" or even kill your plant. Also, if you use fishing line, be careful not to tie the string too tightly around them stem or you could cut into or slice through it.

Advanced Techniques

Once you have the basics of topping, training, and thinning down, you might want to consider taking your plant manipulation to the next level. Be forewarned, if these techniques are done incorrectly they could severely damage or destroy your plants. However, some growers swear by these methods and have had great success with them, but your results may vary.

Twisting and Cracking

Twisting and cracking is a cool technique. You start by placing both hands on the plant about an inch apart (on the same branch). Then twist your fingers in opposite directions until you feel a slight crack, kind of like when you crack your fingers or cartilage. What you are doing is making a wound inside the plant that eventually will heal into a knot. After this has happened the plant will be able to pull water and nutrient more efficiently through that branch.

It usually takes about a week for the plant to heal and you should be able to see a lump where you cracked the plant. The branch that you crack should look as healthy as the rest and it is still able to take in just as much nutrient, if not more.

Some people also bend the plant in half so the whole branch cracks. This has the same effect as twisting, but you can lose the whole branch if you do it wrong and it takes a little longer to heal. Do not use this technique in the blooming or flowering phase. In this phase, your plant uses a lot of its energy to produce flowers or fruits and it does not have enough energy to regenerate itself as fast.

Splitting your Leaves

This technique should be used when you want your plant to concentrate on rooting. All you have to do is cut a couple of the leaves in half and remember to leave enough whole leaves for your plant to live off of. By doing this you are letting the plant know that the leaf is damaged, therefore your plant will strive to produce more root. Advanced growers use this technique when cloning as well.

Pre-Flower Identification

Preflowers, as opposed to full-blown flowers, generally appear after the fourth week of vegetative growth from seed. Check carefully above the fourth node. Please note that preflowers are very small and are difficult to differentiate without magnification.

Female Plants

The female preflower is pear shaped and produces a pair of pistils. Frequently, the female preflowers do not show pistils until well after the preflowers have emerged. Thus, don't yank a plant because it has no pistils. Pistillate preflowers are located at the node between the stipule and emerging branch.

Also, some female preflowers never produce pistils. A female preflower without pistils is difficult to distinguish from a male preflower. Thus, hermaphrodite issues should not be resolved by the appearance of preflowers, without pistils, on a plant otherwise believed to be a female.

Male Plants

The male preflower may be described as a "ball on a stick." However, its most recognizable feature is its absence of pistils. Sometimes, a male plant will develop mature staminate flowers after prolonged periods of vegetative growth. These appear in clusters around the nodes.

The following image shows a male plant in early flowering. Staminate flowers are located at the node between the stipule and emerging branch.

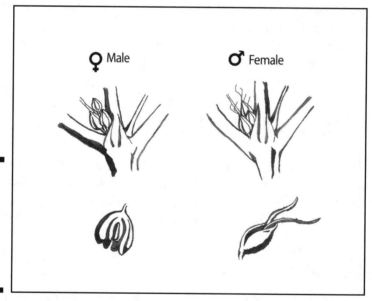

Figure 11-4:
Identifying the sex of your plants is critical in ensuring a seedless crop.

Hermaphrodites

A hermaphrodite is a plant of one sex that develops the sexual organs of the other sex. Most commonly, a flowering female plant will develop staminate flowers, though the reverse is also true. Primarily male hermaphrodites are not as well recognized only because few growers let their males reach a point of flowering where the pistillate would be expressed.

Hermaphrodites are generally viewed with disfavor. First, they will release pollen and ruin a sinsemilla crop, pollinating themselves and all of the other females in the room. Second, the resulting seeds are worthless, because hermaphrodite parents tend to pass on the tendency to their offspring.

Please note that occasionally specious staminate flowers will appear in the last days of flowering of a female plant. These do not drop pollen and their appearance is not considered evidence of deleterious hermaphroditism.

Initiating Flowering

A plant can remain in the vegetative state almost indefinitely under ideal conditions or it can be forced to flower anytime after it has established itself. It is up to the individual and the needs of the garden. If all other conditions remain the same, only the size of the plants, and subsequently the harvest, will be affected by the length of the vegetative period. Keep in mind that a plant can double or even triple in size after it's forced to flower, so plan accordingly.

If you are growing indoors, you will generally want to flower your plants when they are one to three feet tall. Regardless of the size, once you decide to start flowering you must set the lighting cycle to 12/12 (twelve hours of light and twelve hours of darkness). Ten to fourteen days after changing your lighting cycle, your plants will begin to flower. If they haven't already, your plants will begin to show either male pollen sacs or female buds.

You will most likely want to remove the males as soon as they are identified and throw them out or make hash or hash oil out of them. Once they are pulled, the flowering phase has really begun and you will finally see your female plants produce their luscious buds. The length of your flowering phase will vary depending on the strain of marijuana you are growing. It can last anywhere from 39-100 days long, but most indoor (Indica) strains average at about 60 days.

Size *Does* Matter

Regardless of day/night lengths, a plant is only able to produce flowers when it has attained the minimal vegetative size necessary to support the weight of the buds and a sufficient food reserve to supply the considerable demands of developing reproductive organs. Most marijuana plants should be induced to flower no smaller than six inches, but the ideal size is between one and two feet tall for standard indoor growing.

The prize!

Week 2: Vegetative growth continues, with plants growing a third larger before beginning to bud.

Week 3: Vegetative growth ceases as the plant focuses on developing flowers, resin and possibly seeds.

Week 4: Nodes begin to develop buds and increase THC production to protect its seed set.

Week 6: If the plant does not become fertilized, it devotes most of its energy into THC production.

Week 8: Buds continue to grow in size and ripen
as the stigmas turn amber or brown.

Trichomes help prevent seed damage from insects, animals, light degradation and fungal disease.

Perhaps the most successful function of trichomes in plant proliferation is their attractiveness to humans.

To preserve the trichomes on the buds and leaves, wear rubber gloves and handle with care when examining.

Some growers run their THC-covered leaves over a fine mesh screen and then collect the trichomes.

Flushing your plants with distilled water two weeks prior to harvesting reduces the mineral taste.

Harvesting in the morning ensures that your plants will be at peak THC content.

Most growers harvest when 70-90% of the stigmas turn amber and wither to ensure high THC levels.

A pocket microscope works well for getting a closer peek at your trichome development.

Deprive your plants of water for six to twelve hours before harvesting to speed the drying time of your bud.

Cutting medium-sized branches lets you manicure many buds at one time without straining your hands.

Hanging your buds is an effective way to dry them, but it doesn't increase their potency.

Step 1: Find an ideal area to cut, then firmly hold the stem above the cut so the cola doesn't fall to the ground.

Step 2: Make the cut and remove the cola. Gently place branches on wax paper as you harvest the rest of the plant.

Step 3: Begin manicuring the colas by removing the large fan leaves, then clip the smaller leaves near the buds.

Step 4: Use the tips of your bonsai scissors to remove the remaining leaf tips without many trichomes on them.

Step 5: Finally, cut the branch into smaller segments. The buds are then ready to dry or can be further manicured.

When your blades become coated in resin, scrape them off using a razor blade or use rubbing alcohol to clean them.

Female flowers consists of two white stigmas attached at the base to an ovule contained in a tiny green pod.

The ovule is formed from modified leaves (bracts and bracteoles) which envelop the developing seed.

When seed pods open, you can begin to remove the seeds and dry them in a light-proof container.

Seed color and pattern are affected naturally by the need for camouflage.

Sage 'n Sour
Mostly Sativa
Flowering time: 63-70 days

Purp
Sativa 50% / Indica 50%
Flowering time: 60-65 days

Space Queen
Mostly Indica
Flowering time: 50-55 days

Orange Velvet
Mostly Sativa
Flowering time: 60-65 days

Neon Super Skunk
Mostly Indica
Flowering time: 56-63 days

Heavy Duty Fruity
Sativa 50% / Indica 50%
Flowering time: 60-65 days

Kushage
Mostly Sativa
Flowering time: 66-70 days

MK-Ultra
Mostly Indica
Flowering time: 56-63 days

Dutch Dragon
Mostly Sativa
Flowering time: 63-70 days

Swiss Bliss
Mostly Sativa
Flowering time: 63-70 days

Nebula (Close up)
Sativa 55% / Indica 45%
Flowering time: 60-65 days

Sugar Babe
Mostly Indica
Flowering time: 54-60 days

Rox
Mostly Indica
Flowering time: 56-60 days

Sensi Star
Sativa 10% / Indica 90%
Flowering time: 56-63 days

Belladonna
Sativa 50% / Indica 50%
Flowering time: 60 days

Sheherazade
Mostly Indica
Flowering time: 56-60 days

Durga Mata
Effect: Body relaxing with medical qualities

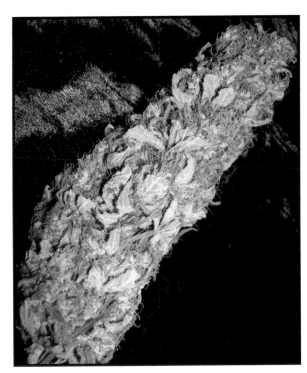

Orange Velvet
Effect: Sweet tasting and energetic

Belladonna
Effect: Trippy

Nebula
Effect: Cerebral, trippy

Dutch Dragon
Effect: A nice clear high with relaxing effects.

Jacks Cleaner
Effect: Smooth taste with a pleasant buzz.

Pinky
Effect: Long lasting, invigorating effects.

Freshly harvested Sputnik 1.0 bud
before drying has begun.

Sputnik 1.0 trimmed to a connoisseur cut and dried
for over a week. Bud is ready to be stored or smoke.

The Orange Velvet strain is over 20 years old and
sports deep shades of burgundy and maroon.

Carefully handling buds after manicuring and drying,
helps maintain high amounts of THC content.

Most growers go for the "connoisseur cut" when manicuring their personal bud.

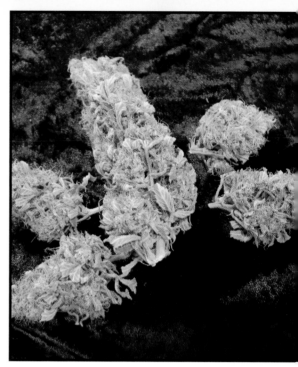

Due to the effort involved, most growers leave some small leaves on the rest of their crop.

Loose buds can be laid out to dry, rather than hanging.

Once the buds are dry, they can be sealed in jars for many months, even years.

Chapter 12

Clones and Mother Plants

• •

In This Chapter

▶ Cloning to determine plant sex

▶ Developing mother plants

▶ Getting the right equipment

▶ Step-by-step cloning

• •

Cloning is the general term for asexual reproduction, which means replicating a plant into many genetic duplicates. When you clone a plant, you take cuttings from an established "mother" plant, usually in vegetative growth, and root them to create many individual plants. The newly created offspring are genetically identical to the mother, including the same sex. Clones can be grown vegetatively and flowered just like a plant grown from seed except since they are usually all female plants, you can almost ensure a sinsemilla (seedless) harvest.

Effective cloning allows you to quickly fill a closet with genetic duplicates of your favorite plants. So when you find a plant you want to be a mother, you can keep that plant's genetic character alive for years. A clone can be taken from a clone at least twenty times, probably more, so don't worry about myths of reduced vigor.

Cloning is not as easy as starting from seed. With seeds, you can have 18-inch plants in four weeks or less. With clones, it may take four weeks just for the plants to sprout roots and new growth to begin. Seeds are easily twice as fast if you have empty indoor space being wasted that needs to be put to use quickly.

Clone Potency

Clones and clones from clones retain their potency. Single lines have been reproduced asexually by cloning for more than twenty years with no loss of potency, odor, or taste. However, the question of genetic drift over many generations is not unreasonable.

Mutations occur on a regular basis in asexual as well as sexual reproduction. Genetic researchers have discovered that genes jump around on chromosomes and recent studies have proved that they also jump from plant to plant. Thus the variety can gradually shift over a period of time.

Clones propagated over many generations along separate lines will look slightly different. Perhaps the answer is to preserve the mother plant for as long as possible – but even a single plant will exhibit some drift. Remember that during sexual reproduction mutations are more likely to occur than during the asexual reproductive process of cloning.

Viruses sometimes attack cannabis. They can affect the plants' health, growth, and potency, as well as affecting the genetic makeup of the plant. Once a plant is infected with a virus, it can never recover. For that reason, more than one plant of a special line should be maintained.

For all its faults, cloning plants is the best way to preserve a plant's particular characteristics with the fewest genetic changes.

Cloning to Determine Sex

As compared to the observation of preflowers, force flowering clones is an almost foolproof method of determining sex. This method assumes that the grower has started a batch of plants from seed and wants to find out which are male and which are female before flowering them or using them as mother plants.

Either way, the point of determining sex through clones is to enable the grown-from-seed plants to continue to grow vegetatively until their clones determine which are male and which are female. Once that's determined, you can eliminate the males and concentrate on flowering or cloning the remaining females.

After several weeks of vegetative growth, the grown-from-seed plants should have branched enough so that cuttings may be taken. The cuttings should have at least one node and be at least two inches tall. Along with the step-by-step instructions in this chapter, follow the instructions below to successfully clone for sex.

1. Number the grown-from-seed plants or otherwise make them distinguishable from each other.

2. Take two cuttings from each seed plant and root them by following the Step-by-Step instructions. Each of these are given the same number as their parent plant to later identify them.

3. Place one clone of each pair into a separate light-proof flowering area with a 12/12 light cycle. Note that these clones will be discarded after they show sex, so nearly any type of light can be used.

4. Optional: The other set of clones can be placed in vegetative growth with the original grown-from seed plants. By the time the flowering clones show sex, the now-identified-as-female vegetative clones are sexually mature and ready to flower themselves or can be used as "mother" plants.

If you give your clones ten hours of light and fourteen hours of uninterrupted darkness, they will indicate their sex faster than if given the standard 12/12 light cycle. Depending on variety and environmental conditions, cuttings will reveal their gender in seven days to two weeks on a 12/12 cycle. On a 10/14 cycle, the time will be reduced by a few days and you'll also save on electricity.

Mother Plants

If you start out by growing from seed, the best way to find a good mother plant is to grow many plants from a single strain. Then, flower test plants to find the qualities you want to reproduce in large quantity. If you are starting out with a clone you got from another trusted grower, you have saved yourself many months prep time. You can start growing the clone out and pruning it into a mother plant in about two months.

Choosing Mother Plants

Plants that are sick, weak, bug-infested or abused are already half-dead and they can't be expected to supply successful cuttings. The reason is that cuttings are cut off from their food supply and must draw on their internal reserves to survive and grow new roots. The fact is, cuttings will go downhill everyday until they have new roots and start to take up nutrients. Clones from vigorous, healthy plants are much better equipped to survive and grow roots than clones from problem plants.

Figure 12-1:
Mother
plants
should be
at least two
months old.

Can I clone a flowering plant?
Yes, but a cutting taken while the mother plant is flowering will need to be forced back to a vegetative state under 24-hour light. This causes additional stress, which slows growth and development.

Rooting may take up to three times longer when the cuttings are taken during the flowering cycle. The cutting may not have enough stored nutrients or carbohydrates to survive. If you must clone a flowering plant, make sure to take the cutting when the mother plant is only a week or two into the flowering phase.

Desirable Characteristics

If you've grown your potential mothers from seed, it can be difficult to know which plants will produce the best clones. Your best bet is to keep all of the vigorously growing females and create a set of clones from each. Make sure to mark them so that you know which clones came from each mothers, then grow them all as you normally would through the flowering phase.

Keep notes on the development of each set of clones and harvest them separately. All things being equal, one or two mothers should rise above the rest in terms of growth rate, pest resistance, ease of cloning, fastest finisher, and best high. Isolate the best mothers and either flower the rest of turn them into hash. You can then clone the mother(s) to create an entire set of genetically identical mothers to ensure you have enough clones for a full growing cycle.

Cloning Equipment

Effective cloning requires an almost completely different set of tools and growing equipment. This is mainly due to the fragile nature of forcing a cutting to develop an entire root system in order to survive. Luckily, most of what you will need is available at a local gardening center and doesn't require any covert buying trips to a hydroponics store.

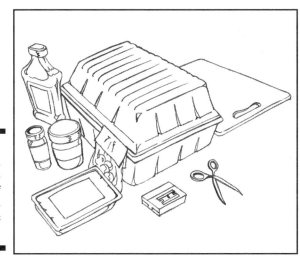

Figure 12-2:
Cloning is a discipline unto itself and requires specific equipment.

For some growers, cloning will be the key to keeping high quality, seedless buds flowing from their grow room. Because of this, the following equipment is essential. Even the best growers have a percentage of clones that just won't root. Keeping your rooting percentage high depends on having quality gear.

- **Unused razor blade(s)**
  Cleanly slices the clone from the mother plant without crushing the stem. Also used to scar the tip of the clone's stem in order to promote faster root growth.

- **Quality trimming scissors**
  Trims excess leaves from clones and splits/halves remaining leaves. Scissors should not be substituted for razor blades as they can pinch the stem and cut off a clone's water supply.

- **Cutting board**
  Used to make additional cuts to the clone stem after removing it from the mother. Also helps when gently scarring the cutting's stem.

- **One-inch starter cubes (Rockwool, Peat, Cocofiber)**
  The medium the clones are placed into after being clipped from the mother. Cubes are available in different mediums and can be purchased in single units or in multipacks that fit perfectly into trays.

- **Slotted tray / solid tray**
  Holds the water that the medium sits in, which is supplied to the roots when needed. Also supplies moisture to the air with the help of a humidity dome and heating pad.

- **"High hat" humidity dome**
  Limits transpiration and keep the medium from drying out. The "high hat" version is the tallest of the three sizes available and easily accommodates four inch clones with room to grow.

🌿 **Fluorescent lighting**
Low wattage/low heat lighting that promotes vegetative growth as the roots develop. Specialized tubes are available specifically for cloning, but are usually unnecessary.

🌿 **Isopropyl rubbing alcohol**
Used to cleans your tools between each cutting.

🌿 **Rooting gel**
Contains hormones that encourage the cutting to grow roots by reducing stress and wilting.

🌿 **Heating mat**
A 40w plastic mat that slightly warms the bottoms of the starter cubes, encouraging root development.

Step by Step Cloning

Now that you've had an overview of how clones are created and know about all of the equipment you need, it's time to get started. The following step-by-step approach is fairly easy to follow and gives all the basics on each step in the process. There are actually many different ways to create clones, but only one has been included to keeps things simple and straightforward.

Step 1: Prepare mothers for cloning

Mother plants should be healthy, pest/disease-free, and at least two months into their vegetative phase. Clones can be taken from mother plants that are less than two weeks into the flowering phase, but these clones will experience shock when forced back to vegetative growth and are often difficult to root.

Foliar feed your mother plants 3-4 days prior to cloning to encourage lush and healthy shoot growth. Also consider using a foliar feeding additive like Growth Plus (a nitrozyme kelp extract containing growth hormones and vitamins) to further accelerate growth.

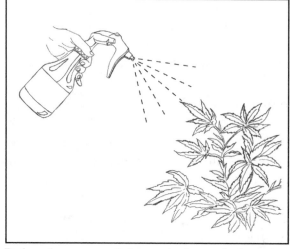

Figure 12-3:
Foliar
feeding
cleans
stomata
pores.

Reduce the amount of nitrogen in the mother's nutrient solution three days prior to cloning by flushing the mother with fresh water. Nitrogen inhibits root growth, so reducing nitrogen levels in your mother plant will help clones root faster.

Step 2: Prepare your medium

If you don't have any distilled water, fill a large bowl with tap water and let it sit in the refrigerator for a full day. After a day, remove the water from the refrigerator and adjust its pH to around 5.5. You can also add a cloning additive such as SuperThrive, but only add as much as the directions specify. After that, let your cubes soak in the water for a few hours prior to cutting your clones.

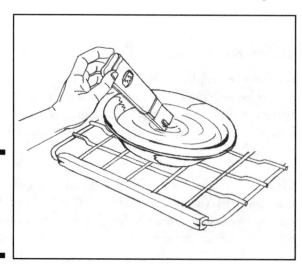

Figure 12-4:
Delicate
clones
require pH
balanced
water.

Step 3: Setting up the equipment

Exposed clones will wilt within a few minutes of cutting them, so it is best to have all necessary materials ready before you start to take cuttings. Dip your scissors and razor blade into alcohol and wipe your cutting board with alcohol. Take your cubes from your water bowl and put them into the grow tray. Use a straw or a chopstick to poke a hole into the cube about halfway down into each one. If you have a heating mat, place it under the grow tray and begin to warm up your medium.

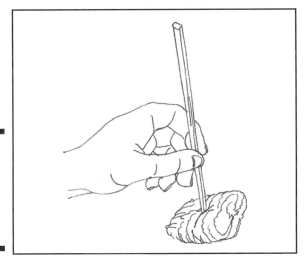

Figure 12-5:
Deepening
the hole in
the rockwool
allows the
cuttings to
fit snuggly.

How clean should my equipment be?

It is critical that you sterilize everything before you start because cuttings are very susceptible to fungus, viruses and diseases until they root. Use rubbing alcohol on your hands, the razor blade and the cutting block. Rinse the shot glass (or whatever you are using) with alcohol, dry it and then fill it ¾ full with rooting hormone.

Step 4: Selecting your clones

Actively growing tops below the main top are preferred, as they contain the most growth hormones. Clones taken from near the bottom of the plant are often spindly and less developed. You should try to locate tops that are around three inches tall with two to three fan leaves and firm, but not woody, stems.

Short clones (no more than two to three nodes) are preferred because they don't have to support large leaves and shoots while also forming roots. The clone should also be "mature" with alternating leaves. Immature clones have leaves opposite each other and are usually pale and spindly.

Some growers do not like to top their moms, preferring to take clones from lower shoots to maintain vertical growth. Lower shoots contain more stored starches, giving the clone more stored energy. Top shoots contain more growth hormones for faster root development. You want to take an equal number of clones from the top and from the bottom and see which root more vigorously with the strains you are growing.

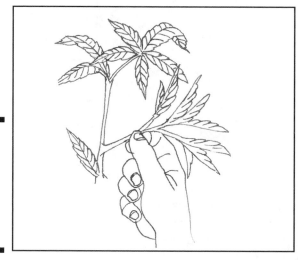

Figure 12-6:
Locate the majority of your cuttings before making any cuts.

As you work through your mother plants to find the ones most suitable for cloning, begin to label them as you go. Whether you use A-B-C, 1-2-3, or a system of your choosing, just remember to label the mothers now and label your clones as you take them. You may also want to add the date and any other special techniques (rooting hormones, top/bottom cutting, scarring/no scarring, etc.) you used when taking the cutting.

When is the best time to cut clones?
During the dark period, plants build up their reserves of water in preparation for the demands of the coming day. By mid-afternoon, water loss from the plant will create water stress in the plant tissues that you would like to use for cutting material. Even a relatively minor water loss will interfere with root development. Of course, the terms "morning" and "afternoon" refer to the plant's timetable—often different than the one outside.

Step 5: Making the cut

Since you have already identified the clones you plan to take, it's just a matter of snipping them. Take one of the growing tops from a mother and use the razor blade to slice it from the main stem—just above a fan leaf—about two nodes from the top. Leave a shoot and a fan leaf on the mother branch to allow it branch into two growing shoots. This is an effective method for "bushing" out your mother plants to ensure you have plenty of branches to clip the next time you need to create clones. If done correctly, you will have twice as many shoots growing than you have clipped off.

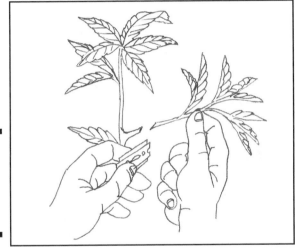

Figure 12-7:
Use a razor blade to make a single, clean cut.

Step 6: Trim the cutting

A leaf stem in a cloning cube will rot—it can't grow roots. To avoid introducing disease into the propagation tray, trim off any leaves near the bottom of the cutting. Cut the leaf stem close to the main stem of the cutting. Leave just a tiny stub of the leaf stem attached to the stem of the cutting. Roots grow from the stub, so it's best to leave a bit so that it's not damaged internally.

Removing the large lower leaves is essential because the cutting has a limited ability to take up water until it grows roots. While some top growth is necessary for the cutting to survive, too many leaves on the cutting place excess demands for water on the stem of the cutting. When cuttings wilt badly and large bottom leaves on the cuttings die off, chances are good that you've left too much foliage on your cuttings.

WEED WARNING

Never tear off the leaf stem from the cutting. This creates a long, ragged wound, which is an open door for disease. Always use a sharp, new razor blade or a pair of clean gardening snips.

Once the top has been cut and the shoots and fan leaves from the lowest nodes have been trimmed, place the clone on the cutting board and use the razor blade to scrape the bottom ½ inch of the shoot. Make sure you scrape, but do not cut.

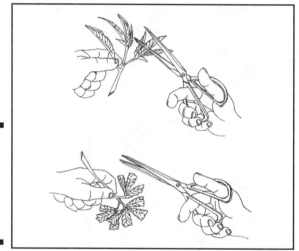

Figure 12-8:
Cut leaves in half to pressure cuttings into rooting faster.

Use the slightest amount of pressure and push the blade to the end, removing a fine outer layer of the stem. Don't hurry, just gently scrape the stem with your blade until you can clearly see the moist internal tissue layers. Finally, cut ¼ inch below the lowest node at a 45° angle to provide a fresh cut before placing it in rooting hormone.

GROWER'S GLOSSARY

Why do I scrape bottom of the shoot/stem?
The purpose of scraping the bottom of the cutting is to scarify the stem so that there is more area in which the cutting can have the opportunity to grow roots and therefore hopefully increase your rooting success rate. Make sure to use a sharp razor blade and a flat surface to scarify the stem.

Step 7: Place the clone in the Medium

Immediately dip the bottom of the cutting into the rooting gel, making sure the lowest node is also coated with gel. Dab any excess gel off of the cut surface itself to avoid suffocating the clone. Now, gently push the stem into the Rockwool or Oasis cube. If the hole is too big, gently squeeze the cube around the stem to seal it.

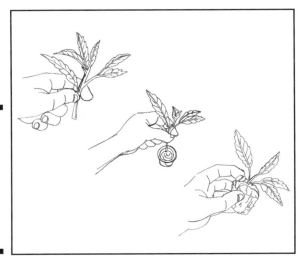

Figure 12-9:
Immediately dip the cutting into a rooting solution and then into a rockwool cube.

You want the cutting planted securely without damaging the stem. Once the cutting is planted into cubes, hold the cube in your hand and gently move it to check that the stem of the cutting is secure. Turn cubes upside down to check that the cutting stem isn't sticking out the bottom. Cuttings that are loose in their grow medium won't root.

Labeling your mom and the clones taken from a particular mom is a good idea to backtrack on a "monster mom". Mark and date all trays, so you know when to expect roots. Try to keep different strains organized in their own trays, watered separately.

Clone Maintenance

By controlling light levels, humidity and temperature, your job is to keep the cutting in a complete state of dormancy. Cuttings without roots are very sensitive to stress. Every effort should be made to minimize evaporation from the cuttings and avoid extreme light and temperature levels. Keep humidity as close to 100% as possible and maintain water and cube temperatures between 70–84°F.

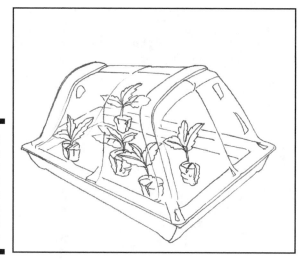

Figure 12-10:
Keep the
humidity
dome on
the tray to
maintain
a humid
environment.

Cooler water slows root formation and warmer water encourages disease. The lower the humidity level, the more water the plant will transpire, causing the cutting to use up stored food for things other than root production. It is important to hold the leaves as dormant as possible and permit the cutting to use more of it's energy on root development.

Checking for Roots

After about a week you can test to see if your plants have started to root. Remove the humidity dome and leave it off for about twenty minutes. Watch the clones for any signs of wilting while the dome is removed. If the plants have not wilted at all, then they probably have enough root development to support themselves. Leave the dome off for another two hours, if they're still standing strong, then you can leave the dome off for good.

On the other hand, if you notice your clones wilting during either of these periods, spray the cuttings and inside the dome and replace the dome over the tray. Try leaving the dome off again in another day or two and eventually the clones will be able to support themselves. Remember to stop misting the cuttings and after you leave the humidity dome off because once plants have roots, constant misting can actually be harmful.

If the lower leaves start to turn yellow and die, don't worry, it is perfectly normal and proof the clone is actively growing. The plant is feeding off of itself to sustain life, moving valuable nutrient and water from the older growth. Unrooted clones often appear healthy and green (and will stay that way for weeks). Never remove any dead growth until the plant is well rooted. If you remove the dying growth the plant can starve and die completely.

Roots should begin to exit the cube in seven to fourteen days. A gentle upward tug on the clone will tell you if it is rooted (only do this after seven days). Unrooted clones will pull out. Roots may be present, but not yet exiting the cube. If in doubt, carefully open the cube.

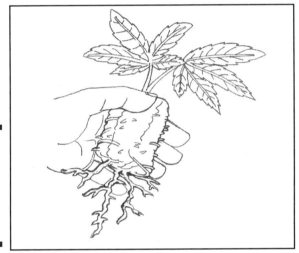

Figure 12-11:
Once roots have grown through the rockwool, it's time to transplant.

If you have a lot clones, sort out the unrooted, few roots, vigorous rooted clones into their own trays. If a clone has not shown roots in two weeks, consider removing it. Roots should be white and fuzzy. Brown roots indicate rot. Occasionally, root tips will become air burned, a sign to water more often.

Begin to increase nitrogen levels by adding weak nutrients (50-200 ppm) to the tray and administer them with water more frequently to avoid drying out the exposed root tips. You could also try a weak foiliar feeding with Growth Plus (or any kelp extract).

Once the clones have fully established roots, they can be put under weak HID light or higher powered lamps that are at least two to three feet above the plants. A weak (250-500 ppm) nutrient regime can be applied or you can transplant them into a hydroponics system.

Troubleshooting your Clones

Successful cloning can require a lot of trial and error, even if you precisely follow all of the directions. There are a lot of variables to consider; more than simply growing and harvesting the plant itself. One day your clones may look fine and the next morning you can find them completely wilted without warning or opportunity to troubleshoot the issue.

By keeping a watchful eye, you may be able to spot problems and prevent any major damage to your fragile cuttings. At the very least, reviewing these trouble spots can help you prevent some of the more common problems before they ever occur.

✓ Make clones are firmly seated in the medium. If they are too firmly seated, you may have bent or broken the stem and hindered water uptake.

✓ Make sure that the lights aren't too bright, fluorescents are all that's needed. An anti-transpirant spray will greatly reduce wilting—they form a waxy barrier that keeps water inside the cutting.

✓ The cuttings may be too large with too much leaf mass. You can trim off half of each leaf to reduce area or take smaller cuttings.

✓ Closely monitor the ambient air temperature. Anything above 80°F is too hot and will accelerate both transpiration and the drying out of your medium.

Transplanting Clones

When your clones have developed plenty of white healthy roots of about two to three inches long, they should be ready to transplant to your hydroponics system. Start by setting your rockwool or oasis cubes in the bottom of your larger pots with the baby plant sticking straight up. Lightly apply grow rocks, loose Rockwool, or any other medium you have decided on, around the Rockwool or Oasis cube until it is completely covered and the pot is full. If possible, add some vitamin B-1 or transplant nutrient to your reservoir take to insure that your baby plants will survive the transplant.

Transplanting Into Flowering

You can definitely transplant clones directly into the flowering phase, but they won't yield much unless they have at least formed an adequate root system. First of all, the term "rooted clone" is pretty misleading in the context of the stories you read about doing SOG (Sea of Green) grows.

To most people, the term "rooted clone" is what it sounds like, a clone that has just formed its roots. The idea of sending a clone into the flowering phase usually means that the clones are "DNA age mature," meaning the clone is technically as old as it's mother and is theoretically ready to flower at any time. However, you're still going to need to grow them vegetatively to develop a more adequate root system.

In the context of SOG grows, the idea of budding a small clone is related to the idea of packing more plants per square foot. The intention is to grow many single spiked "budsickle-style" plants often used in some perpetual harvest methods.

If you desire a rack full of budsickles that look like small tree trunks, you must grow the clones vegetatively for at least a week, sometimes more, before an adequate root system has developed. Without a fully formed root system for the uptake of water an nutrients, the plant won't be able to develop or support any large tops.

It should be noted that roots will continue to grow after clones are forced to flower, but in order to get a good start in budding, the clone must have a sufficiently developed root system before flowering is initiated. Plants with well-developed root system in place *before* flowering will always give you bigger and better buds.

Chapter 13

Flowering

In This Chapter

▶ Lighting and feeding during the flowering phase

▶ Understanding the dark period

▶ Flushing your grow medium before harvesting

▶ Selecting the right time to harvest your plants

Flowering is the third and final phase of the marijuana plant's cycle of life. Marijuana grown outdoors automatically begins to flower in the fall due to shorter days and longer nights. This increased dark period signals the marijuana plant's chemistry to change. Vegetative growth begins to slow and energy is focused on producing flowers, seeds, and most importantly, THC.

As the plants begin to flower, male plants will produce pollen and female plants will produce ovules. Hermaphrodites produce both types of flowers. In nature, the pollen drifts from the male plants and onto the female plants, where it moves down the pistil of the female plant and into the ovule, where pollination occurs. Once a plant has been pollinated, it concentrates all of its energy into producing seeds. Once seeds are created, its life cycle is complete and the plant withers and dies.

When growing indoors, the flowering phase is dramatically different than when growing naturally outdoors. First, you determine when the plant begins to flower, not the season. Second, if you have removed all of the male plants and any possibility of pollen reaching your female plants, they will never become pollinated and never produce seeds. These two techniques, forced flowering and seedless flowering, are what make indoor growing so attractive. You can harvest plants up to six times a year and your harvests contain no seeds.

Nutrients

Since you have already introduced nutrients to your plants, you don't have to gradually introduce them, but since you are changing the type of nutrients, you should introduce them at half strength for a few days before increasing them to full strength.

While the amount of overall nutrients you supply will remain the same, the type of fertilizers you use must change. While plants are growing vegetatively, they require more nitrogen to propel growth. As you change the lighting cycle to initiate flowering, your plants need less nitrogen and more phosphorus. Heightened levels of nitrogen during the flowering phase will actually delay flowering and stunt bud production, so switching nutrients is essential, not optional.

You should buy a bloom formula with an N-P-K value of 15-30-30. This strength of fertilizer promotes healthy budding and increases potency. You should still supply water to your plants three to six times per day, depending on plant size and other factors. Remember not to overfertilize or you will end up burning your plants.

If you have room for additional vegetative growth, consider introducing your flowering nutrients one to two weeks after you have changed the lighting cycle. As you will learn later in this chapter, marijuana plants continue to grow vegetatively for up to two weeks after changing the lighting cycle. If you want more growth before budding begins, keep feeding your plants vegetative nutrients, then switch to flowering nutrients as soon as your plants show signs of flowering.

Lighting

When you are ready to flower your plants, you want to make sure to change your lighting cycle as well as your nutrients. When you grow your plants in the vegetative phase, you want them to receive 18 to 24 hours of light each day. When you want to initiate flowering you must change the light cycle so that your plants will get a solid twelve hours of light and, more importantly, a solid twelve hours of darkness each day. This lighting cycle will activate the flowering or budding phase.

Light Type

You can use any of the three main types of lighting (high-pressure sodium, metal halide, or fluorescent) for the flowering phase. However, high-pressure sodium (HPS) bulbs are much more efficient for this phase. The HPS bulb emits an orange-red spectrum lighting, which is ideal for the flowering phase.

HPS bulbs have an advantage over other types of bulbs in that they help increase yield, resin glands, and oil essence in your plants. For complete information on all of your lighting options, review the Lighting chapter.

Night Lengths

Plants are able to measure the passage of time and thereby set in motion their reproduction processes. Specifically, plants measure night lengths, rather than daylight hours, so keep in mind that it is more crucial that your plants get twelve hours of uninterrupted darkness rather than twelve hours of light.

Some strains of marijuana require different lengths of darkness to induce flowering based largely on the origination of the strain and various breeding practices. The majority of strains available from seed distributors adhere to 12/12 cycles and would definitely indicate if it were otherwise. Some equatorial-based varieties may not be light cycle triggered at all. This means that they are used to growing under 12/12 all the time and will flower (and finish) when they genetically programmed to.

If you extend the light period by an hour or two (13/11 to 14/10) you can correspondingly extend the flowering period by 10 to 15% (usually ten to fourteen days). There is an added bulk that makes up for the extended time, but the buds may be a bit leafier. However, remember that any attempts to use a cycle that does not add up to 24 hours should be considered very experimental as it goes against the natural rhythm that the plant has evolved with.

Making it Dark

Consider that cannabis can flower outdoors under the light of the full moon, so if your grow room is that dark, you should be fine. Having said that, it's best to make it as dark as possible. Plug all light leaks and be liberal with the black plastic and duct tape.

Be sure to let your eyes adjust to the darkened room for at least two minutes before you try and identify how "truly dark" it is. If you can hold your hand out at arm's length and see your fingers, then it is probably too bright. Light leaks are common triggers for hermaphrodite plants and stunted growth. For more information on making your grow room "light tight," review the Safety and Security chapter.

Dark Period Accidents

If low-powered light reaches your plants for a minute or two, you probably didn't do too much damage, but watch the situation closely for a while. Stress of this kind can cause hermaphrodites to develop. It may only appear on a few buds, so keep a very close lookout. If this doesn't happen, you've only set them back a week or so. They should continue to flower and finish as expected, but it will just take a little longer than usual.

Vegetative Growth While Flowering

Regardless of strain, the growth or stretch after switching to 12/12 will continue for about a third of the entire length of the flowering cycle. So if they complete flowering in eight weeks, you have at least two and half weeks of vertical growth to contend with after initiating flowering.

If your plants are already at full size when you initiate flowering, you should tie the top shoots down immediately. You don't have many other options if the plants are too tall for your space and you're already flowering. It's too late to trim them back and if you can't raise the light or lower the plants, so you have to tie them down.

Use string or a long roll of bendable twist ties and attach one end to the top of the branch you want to tie down. Attach the other end to some good staking points either on the plant containers or in the tray and pull down the tallest shoots until they are at a manageable canopy level. They will revert back to top growth and be pointing up a few hours after tying them down. You won't get the big top colas that you normally would, but you will likely increase your yield given the circumstances.

Pruning Leaves While Flowering

A raging debate exists as to whether it is appropriate to remove fan leaves from flowering plants in order to get more light to lower bud sites. Two distinct schools of thought have emerged:

First, there are those that say that if a fan leaf is blocking a lower bud it should to be removed. These buds cannot develop as well because their light is being blocked.

Second, there are those that say that the fan leaves, whether they are blocking bud sites or not, are the plant's primary solar collectors. Remove these and you are taking away the plant's ability to gather light and convert it into energy. Moreover, the fan leaves store sugars that the plant needs for bud development. When a plant has no more need for a leaf, it will fall off on its own.

Finally, a compromise is possible between the two methods: the upper fan leaves may be pared in half to permit light to the lower buds and lower fan leaves may be tucked so that light penetrates to the lower bud sites. The leaves can still collect light and act as a food source for the buds without blocking bud sites. Incorporating both methods is highly recommended.

Look But Don't Touch

You shouldn't handle your buds as they flower. If you squeeze or twist your buds, you are causing them to prematurely die. Sometimes they recover and grow around the affected area, sometimes they don't. Use your eyes to judge the size. Just remember, don't be hasty, waiting makes it tasty.

If you enjoy sniffing a sample (or taste) of the resin, it's best to take it from a sugary leaf protruding from the bud. It's easy to remove some crystals by rubbing a leaf blade between your thumb and forefinger and smelling them to give you an indication of the enjoyment you'll soon be experiencing.

Flushing the Medium

Much time and thought has been put into the feeding needs of each part of marijuana's life cycle, yet for some reason the final stages of resin development always seem to be ignored. The vegetative period of plant growth only sets the platform for the trichome production that you're after.

Since you are most likely using a chemical fertilizer in your hydroponics reservoir, you should clear the nutrients from your plants during the last one to two weeks of flowering. This helps the plant to use the nutrient reserves stored in its foliage. The lack of nutrients forces the plants to use the extra nitrogen and other elements stored in their tissues, which helps your bud to taste better. Plants that have been properly flushed before harvesting have no harsh chemical or "green" taste from excess chlorophyll, nitrogen, and other elements in the final smoke.

There are two different ways that you can rinse and flush your plants. The first and most common way is to just give your plant cold water for the last two weeks with no added nutrients. You will want to pump out all of the nutrient solution in your reservoir and even consider giving it a thorough cleaning and then replace the solution with cold water. Of course, you will probably need to adjust the pH using natural or commercial adjusters, but you should add no additional nutrients.

The second way is to buy a rinsing or flushing solution. Most of the rinsing and flushing solutions that you will buy are far better than just using pure water. These also increase resin glands and oil essence in your buds. What these additives do is imitate nature, allowing the plant to absorb limited amounts of nutrient and water so the plant thinks that it is the end of the season. The plant will know that it is in its last weeks of blooming or fruiting and will produce as much bud and resin as it can before the season is over.

Determining Peak Harvest Time

There are several important points to consider when deciding exactly when to harvest your cannabis crop. There is a difference in harvest times between Sativas and Indicas in bloom duration and final effect. There is a difference between early and late harvest to encourage head to body high, respectively. There is the issue of chemistry, because what we are really considering in terms of "ripeness" relates directly to the chemical nature and state of the plant at harvest. Finally, there is the concept of "the window of harvest," which is where we will begin.

The Window of Harvest

The window of harvest is the period during which the plant is at its optimum state of ripeness. The window "opens" when the plant is first ripe. Somewhere along the way the plant becomes over-ripe, which signifies the "closing" of the window of harvest.

For most Indicas grown indoors, the window of harvest is about two weeks long, give or take a couple of days for various strains. If going directly from an 18/6-hour vegetative light cycle to a 12/12-hour bud cycle, most Indicas take about eight weeks to fully mature.

For Sativas grown indoors, the window may be open much longer. Some Sativas take up to thirteen weeks to mature indoors.

Head High or Body Stone?

An important consideration has to do with one's preference for a "head" high or more of a "body" high. A good head high can positively influence one's mental state much like a psychedelic; whereas a good body high is more similar to a narcotic effect. Generally, head highs tend to be more up and body highs tend to be more down. Suffice it to say that a good healthy mix of the two is a fine goal to achieve.

Sativas and early window harvests tend to be more of a head high, whereas Indicas and late window harvests tend to be more of a body high. Given this rule of thumb you can pretty much come up with what you want. That is, if you prefer a very psychedelic head high, then an early harvested Sativa might do best. If a very narcotic body high is desired, then a late harvest indicas would probably do best. For that best-of-both worlds high, experimentation with late harvested sativas and early-to-mid harvested indicas usually proves interesting.

Determining Plant Maturity

Starting in the third or fourth week of the flowering light cycle, glandular stalked trichomes will begin to form along the surfaces of leaves, flowers, bracts and stems. At the same time, more and more flowers (also called calyxes) develop into densely packed floral clusters.

The pistils of the young flowers are bright white and turn reddish brown with age. The pistils and flowers develop from the bottom of the bud to the top. The older, lower pistils are the first to turn reddish brown. For most basic indicas this usually happens by the sixth week in the flowering cycle. It is about this time that the calyxes begin to swell.

Calyx swelling is a major indicator of peak maturity. The lowest, oldest calyxes swell first and the swelling works its way up to the highest, youngest flowers on each bud. At peak maturity about 90% of the calyxes will almost look seeded because of their lush size. Three quarters to 90% of the pistils will have turned reddish brown as well. For a basic Indica, this takes well into the seventh week of the flowering cycle.

By the end of the eighth week, most of the calyxes will have swollen and a surge of trichome development has coated most of the buds. It is now that the development of a very discerning palate comes into play to determine the best harvest time.

The ripening signs for most Sativas are highly similar, except extended over a longer period of time. Occasionally, some Sativas have windows of peak harvest that actually open and close. That is, for a week or so the plant may exhibit signs of peak ripeness. However, a week later the plant may have a growth spurt, which lowers the trichome-to-fiber ratio and overall potency for a little while. Usually a fibrous growth spurt is accompanied by a corresponding increase in THC production. Again, time and experience are the key elements in this regard.

Magnify Your Buds

Various highs experienced by different harvest times are actually variations in plant chemistry. The chemicals you enjoy when smoking are produced within the glandular stalked trichomes along the surfaces of the bud flowers (calyxes), bracts, leaves and stems, starting in or around the fourth week of the bud cycle. More and more of these trichomes develop as the plant matures.

A small 25x or stronger pocket microscope, which can be picked up inexpensively at electronics stores, works well for getting a closer peek at your trichome development. Use the microscope to examine the capitate stalked glandular trichomes.

The coloration of gland heads can vary between strains and maturity. Most strains start with clear or slightly amber heads, which gradually become cloudy or opaque when THC levels have peaked and are beginning to degrade. Regardless of the initial color of the secretory cavity, with careful observation, you should be able to see a change in coloration as maturity levels off.

Some cultivators wait until about half of the secretory cavities become opaque before harvesting to ensure maximum THC levels in the finished product. Of course nothing tells the truth more than your own perception, so try samples at various stages to see what is best for you and the strain you are growing.

While you may be increasing the total THC level in the bud by allowing half of the glands to go opaque, the bud will also have a larger percentage of THC breakdown products such as CBN, which is why some people choose to harvest earlier while most of the secretory cavities are still clear.

Indica varieties will usually have a ten to fifteen day harvest window to work with. Sativas and Indica/Sativa hybrids often have an extended period to work with. View the buds daily and take smoking samples every few days during the window of harvest to determine the type of high you prefer. Once you find what you're looking for, harvest your crop.

More about Trichomes

Although cannabis resin glands, called trichomes, are structurally diverse, they come in three basic varieties:

⚘ Bulbous (1)

The bulbous type is the smallest (15-30 micron). From one to four cells make up the "foot" and "stalk," and one to four cells make up the "head" of the gland. Head cells secrete a resin - presumably cannabinoids, and related compounds which accumulate between the head cells and the cuticle. When the gland matures, a nipple-like protrusion may form on the membrane from the pressure of the accumulating resin. The bulbous glands are found scattered about the surfaces of the above-ground plant parts.

⚘ Capitate-Sessile (2)

The second type of gland is much larger and is more numerous than the bulbous glands. They are called capitate, which means having a globular-shaped head. On immature plants, the heads lie flush, appearing not to have a stalk and are called capitate sessile. They actually have a stalk that is one cell high, although it may not be visible beneath the globular head. The head is composed of usually eight, but up to 16 cells, that form a convex rosette. These cells secrete cannabinoids, and related compounds which accumulate between the rosette and it's outer membrane. This gives it a spherical shape. The gland measures from 25 to 100 micron across.

⚜ Capitate-Stalked (3)

Cannabinoids are most abundant in the capitate-stalked gland which consists of a tier of secretory disc cells subtending a large non-cellular secretory cavity. During flowering the capitate glands that appear on the newly formed plant parts take on a third form. Some of the glands are raised to a height of 150 to 500 micron when their stalks elongate. These capitate-stalked glands appear during flowering and form their densest cover on the female flower bracts. They are also highly concentrated on the small leaves that accompany the flowers. The male flowers have stalked glands on the sepals, but they are smaller and less concentrated than on the female bracts. Male flowers form a row of very large capitate glands along the opposite sides of anthers.

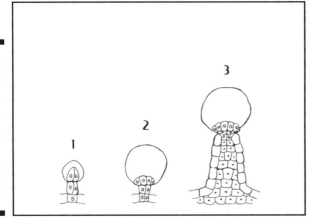

Figure 13-1:
While all trichomes contribute to the "high," an abundance of capitate-stalked trichomes is desired.

Chapter 14

Harvesting

. . . .

In This Chapter

▶ Harvesting your crop step-by-step

▶ Trimming and manicuring your buds

▶ Drying your harvest

▶ Learning the important of curing

. . . .

Harvesting is the reaping of the bounty and is the most enjoyable time you will spend with your garden. Plants are harvested when the flowers are ripe. Generally, ripeness is defined as when the white pistils start to turn brown/orange and start to withdraw back into the false seedpod. The seedpods swell with resins usually reserved for seed production, giving you ripe sinsemilla buds with red and golden hairs.

Most new growers want to pick early, because they are impatient and that's OK. Just take buds from the middle of the plant or the bottom and allow the rest to keep maturing. Often, the older (lower) parts of the plant will ripen first. Harvest them and let the rest of the plant continue to ripen. You will notice the top buds getting bigger and fuzzier as they come into full maturity.

Use a magnifier and try to see the capitate stalked trichomes (little THC crystals on the buds). If they are mostly clear, not brown, the peak of floral bouquet is near. Once they are mostly all turning brownish in color, the THC levels are dropping and the flower is past optimum potency, declining rapidly with light and fan. However, don't harvest too late! It's easy to be too careful and harvest so late that potency has declined. Watch the plants and learn to spot peak floral potency.

Getting ready to cut

It's up to you to decide how much time you want to spend manicuring and how much you care about the quality and appearance of the finished product. The following are instructions for the clean cut or connoisseur-style manicure as well as tips on other ways of cutting along the way. First, a little about the preparations you must take before tackling your first manicuring session.

Gather Your Tools

You will need paper towels, rubbing alcohol or vegetable/olive oil, razor blades, newspaper/wax paper, and sharp scissors to get the job done. Trimming scissors are the most important type of scissors you will need, since the entire job can be done with these scissors alone. Many growers use specialty scissors made for bonsai growers because they are super sharp, lightweight, and have small blades for easy maneuvering. You might also want to consider using pruning scissors to cut large branches and fan leaves.

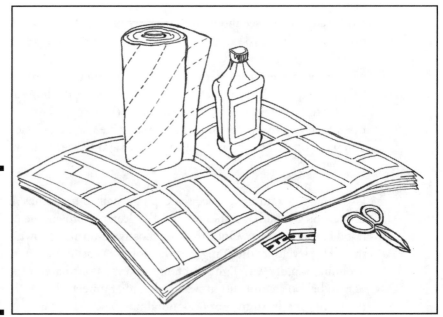

Figure 14-1: Lay your equipment out before you start to ensure you have everything you need.

Whichever type of scissors you choose, you will want your trimming blades to move freely from the start and have comfortable handles. Some specialty scissors are spring loaded and make it easier to work through hours of clipping. Some growers like these, others don't, the point is to find something that's comfortable and durable enough to allow you to manicure for hours.

Choosing a Cutting Spot

Manicuring can take a long time depending on the size of your crop, so pick a comfortable spot for the job because you will most likely spend hours trimming in the same position. It can take over ten hours to manicure a pound of marijuana, give or take a few hours, depending on how you cut and how fast you work. It takes considerably less time for commercial-type cuts and even less for a quick strip cut. You may find the quality of your manicuring quickly slipping after a few hours on the job if you're uncomfortable while performing the work.

Prepare Your Space

Make sure you have everything you need close by and lay some newspaper or even better, wax paper, down on the surface you're using. You want to keep your working surface clean to make it easier move leaves and bud when the surface is covered. You also want everything you need to be close by so you won't have to go searching for it later when your hands are covered in sticky resin. Now that you've gathered your tools and picked a spot to cut, you're ready to get to work.

Instead of using newspaper or wax paper, some growers manicure over a glass table, if available, so they can collect the trichomes that falls off the plant while cutting. Resin can be easily scraped off a glass table using a credit card. You can find many uses for this wonderful by-product.

Cutting Down Your Plants

Begin by selecting the plants you want to harvest, then chop them down one at a time. Remove the plant from the grow room and then cut the branches into workable sections and place them on your work area. If you are just doing a strip job, that's all the cutting you need to do aside from separating the buds from the branches.

Part III: The Grow

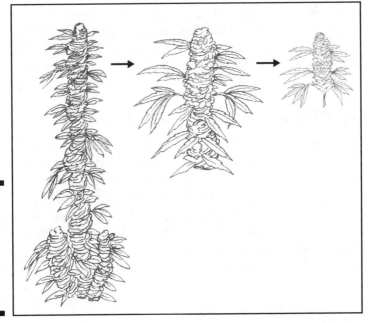

Figure 14-2:
Break down
your plants
until you can
comfortably
hold each
bud in your
hand.

How small should I shop the plants before manicuring?
When breaking down a single plant into manageable branches, you want
the branches to be a size that's easy to handle. Not so long that they sag,
but not so short that you are working with too many branches that are
hard to get a grip on with your fingers.

Quick Cut

If you are going for the quickest trim possible, you can simply run a
gloved hand down each branch to remove most of the large fan leaves. Of
course the majority of the plant's leaves and stems remain, but if you can't
devote time to proper a manicure, that shouldn't be much of a concern.

To even consider leaving so much excess leaf on your buds you have to
be looking at many pounds of marijuana, meaning many long days of
trimming work, to even consider this method. All of the dried, crumbly
leaves left on your high-quality marijuana makes it look less than
desirable and can add a mineral, vegetative taste to your smoke.

Manicuring

Hopefully you have decided to spend the time and effort to properly manicure your buds instead of the quick cut. If so, your plants should now be cut into manageable branches and ready for a finer trim. You can start to remove the large fan leaves, branch by branch, and then use the spin move for the smaller bud leaves.

Step 1: Removing fan leaves

Cut the fan leaves off at the stem as close to the branch as possible for the clean cut. For fan leaves growing out of the bud you have two choices. For a clean cut, a little bit of maneuvering of the bud with your snip blade tips is called for whenever you can't get to the stem or you could just make the cut at buds edge.

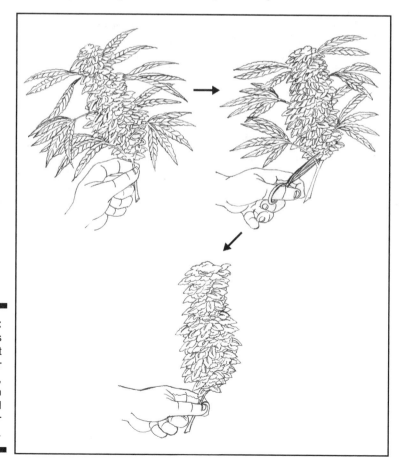

Figure 14-3:
Fan leaves aren't suitable for smoking, but can be used in hash or butter.

Mastering the Spin Move

Spinning a bud's stem between your fingers as you cut the leaves is a powerful technique to use to avoid excessive hand cramps. Start by grabbing the bud stem with your thumb and forefinger so you can easily spin the bud 360 degrees. As you spin, use your other fingers to guide and stabilize the bud as you cut, enabling you to keep working without having to adjust the bud for cutting. With the spin move you can keep snipping by moving the bud leaves towards the cutting blades instead of contorting the blades to reach every possible bud leaf.

Step 2: Clipping the bud leaves

Bud leaves are the single-bladed leaf tips growing directly out of your bud. These tiny leaves can be difficult to clip without also mangling your buds. To avoid this, continue using your trimming scissors and use the spin move. The leaves closest to the bud are covered with resin, so keep them for making hash or for smoking.

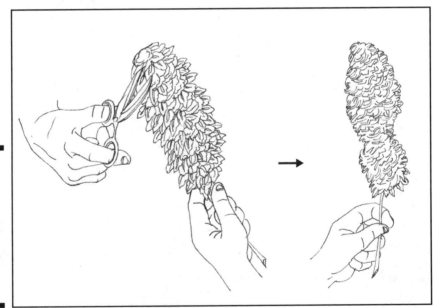

Figure 14-4:
Examine the bud leaves before snipping, they may be worth leaving on if covered in trichomes.

As you start trimming the bud leaves, you must make a decision on how much leaf to leave on the bud? A connoisseur will take it all off except maybe leaving the completely resin-coated leaves. Typical stoners will leave anything with a decent amount of resin. A lazy and/or commercial grower will leave them all on—it's up to you.

Step 3: Removing bud from branch

The last major step is to separate the buds from the branch. For smaller buds, the trimming scissors come in handy since the stems are thin. For bigger stems, you may want to use larger, heavy-duty scissors.

Before you make the final clip, you need to decide how much stem to leave on the bud and when you should separate a big bud into smaller buds. The decision is yours, but remember that the more stem you leave, the longer it will take to dry and in the end, nobody wants to smoke stems anyway. On whatever bud size you decide to cut to, you should always leave a bit of a handle to hold on to without smashing the bud.

As far as the harvesting and manicuring of your buds, you're done. Now all you have to do is dry the bud and any leaf you kept for cooking, smoking, and/or hash making.

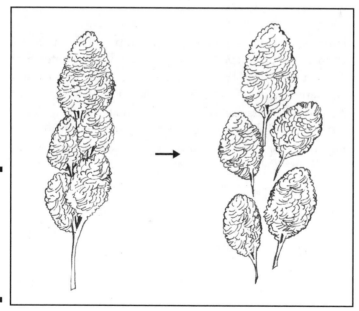

Figure 14-5:
Nugget-sized buds are easy to store and decrease mold development.

Cleaning

Cleaning your tools isn't something you will only do when you are done harvesting your crops. Depending on how resinous your plants are, you will likely have to clean your tools multiple times as you cut and manicure.

As you clip through thousands of leaves, your scissor blades will become sticky with resin and a quick cleaning is necessary to keep the blades sharp and frictionless. You can use a razor to scrape lengthways down your scissor blades to peel off the resin coating. These scrapings are commonly known as "scissor hash" and it *can* be smoked. You can use alcohol or vegetable/olive oil to clean your hands of resin.

When you have finished manicuring for the day, use a razor blade and some rubbing alcohol for the final cleaning. Soak a paper towel with the alcohol and use the paper towel to wipe your blades completely clean. Use as much alcohol as you need to since the more you use, the easier it is to clean your scissors. You could also soak your tools in alcohol and wipe them down a few hours later, which is less time consuming.

Drying Your Harvest

Both drying and curing require precise control of the speed and rate at which moisture is removed from your buds. The drying of your harvest should be a slow, steady process of allowing the water to evaporate from the vegetative matter. The amount of time it takes to dry your buds depends on several factors: density of the material being dried, atmospheric conditions in and around the drying area (temperature and humidity), and the amount of air circulation in the area. Before drying you should have already trimmed all unwanted leaf material while the flowers were fresh.

Do not cure pot in the sun because it greatly reduces potency. It is recommended that you slow cure your buds by hanging them upside down in a dark, ventilated space. Drying in a paper bag works too and may be much more convenient. Bud tastes great when slow dried over the course of a week or two.

Typical places to dry are attics, closets, dresser drawers, and basements. The best position for a bud to dry in is hanging upside down in a location where air can circulate all around it. If you are fortunate to have a location that you can do this in, great, otherwise use a dresser drawer or some other concealed location.

If you dry the buds in dresser drawers remember not to double stack the buds or the weight of the upper layer of buds will cause a flat spot on the buds underneath. Also remember to rotate the buds every day so the herb dries uniformly and to check for signs of mold or fungus.

THC does not drain from the roots down into the buds; THC forms in the resin on the buds. Hanging plants upside down by the roots will not increase the potency of your buds, but it will greatly delay the time it takes to dry your them.

The entire drying process should take place over one to two weeks depending on the size and variety of bud, the temperature, and the relative humidity of the drying area. If the buds are dried too quickly, the flavor of the herb will become harsh. If the pot is dried too slowly, then molds and fungi may develop and have a similar effect.

With any method of drying, the process must be monitored on a day-to-day basis. Room temperature is fine for drying as long as the humidity is kept low. If drying must take place in a cool damp area, a fan and possibly a heater should be installed to compensate.

Dry buds until the stems are brittle enough to snap and then cure them in a sealed Tupperware container, burping air and turning the buds daily for two weeks.

Quick-Dry Methods

Some growers strongly discourage other growers from sampling buds that haven't been properly dried and cured. Others think it's a good way to tell when your herb has reached its peak. The following methods are for "quick drying" purposes only and results should not be compared to cannabis that has been dried and cured properly. Also, buds that are removed before maturity will reduce your plants potential yield.

Remember, the traditional way of air-drying your buds is the best way to dry and cure is certainly advised. Additionally the ideal way to smoke buds right off the plant would be a vaporizer.

To all those first trying these methods, I would urge patience and multiple attempts. It can be difficult to get any of them right the first time, but keep trying.

Oven

Quick drying in the oven does work and you can smoke the end result. Taste and potency decline to next to nothing, but smoke will go out of your mouth as you exhale. If that's all you crave, then this is the simplest way to dry your herbs out; just keep an eye on it. Many find oven-dried weed to be lacking in everything, including the high.

Microwave

When used on lower power settings (40-50%), a microwave can do an adequate quick-dry job. The bud can still taste like terrible and certainly not as potent as air-dried, but in a pinch it will work. Keep an eye on it and nuke for short five to ten second bursts.

Ballast drying method

First, cut up some fresh buds and spread them out evening in a envelope. Close the envelope and place it on top of your ballast, then leave it on the ballast while the light is on for two to three hours. It may seem like a long time, but after you dry your buds, you can put it in an airtight container and allow the moisture to move from the stem back into the bud. Considering this is a quick-dry method, the taste is usually good and the potency is acceptable.

Step-by-Step Curing

Curing is a process by which the drying process is slowed down, literally to a crawl. You're trying to protect that last bit of precious moisture from evaporation, for this is the magic ingredient of an intense cure. This moisture will use the air in the jar to form aerobic bacteria that will convert (eat) the chlorophyll and cure your buds.

Step 1: Seal your buds

Place your air dried buds into airtight, re-sealable glass jars. Fill the jars up to 80-90% with buds; remembering that the air you leave in the jar is needed to suck up moisture. Every time you open the jar to check for ammonia, you replenish the air supply in the jar, which again removes more moisture.

When buds are jarred at precisely the right time they will regain a moist feeling when you open the jar a few days later. The buds will be moist enough to where you will need to let them dry for a while before sealing them again.

Step 2: Allow the buds to breath

Lay the buds out and let them dry to the point where they seem ready to smoke. Now jar them again and check them in a couple of days. Most likely they've remoistened and this is exactly what you want. The only bad sign is a smell of ammonia, which indicates that you waited too long before opening your jars and your buds became too moist. Too much moisture is like fuel for the bacteria that colonized the flowers.

WEED WARNING

Too much bacterium can ruin your harvest, but some is necessary to convert the chlorophyll (green) in the flowers to a smooth golden brown or red. This bacterium can only be allowed to live in small numbers and must not be allowed to thrive. A little moisture is good, but too much moisture is a bad thing.

Step 3: Squeeze test your buds

Eventually you will open you jars and your buds will no longer be moist, but should be spongy to the touch if lightly squeezed. From this point on, your buds are ready to smoke and will have much of the flavor and potency you expect from great marijuana.

Step 4: Storing your buds

If you want to enhance the flavor and taste even more, you should set aside enough bud to smoke for the next month and place the rest back in the jars. Keep the buds sealed until you need them. As long as the jars are air tight, the buds will continue to cure and you can then dip in for more as needed.

The entire process, from harvest to these first smokable products, can take anywhere from two to eight weeks, depending on your climate. Extremes in climate, such as very arid deserts or tropical humid areas, may take more or less time. There is no substitute for consistent, hands-on checking.

TIPS 'N' TRICKS

Proper curing can exponentially increase the quality and desirability of your harvest. The key word to remember is "slow." You've spent a lot of time and expense to grow your buds, take the extra time to make them the best you can.

Watch for Mold

The main thing to watch (and smell) for throughout the cure process is mold. Whenever mold is found it must be dealt with immediately. The moldy bud needs to be removed, and the rest of the product needs to be exposed to a drier environment for a while.

The simplest solution is to go back one step. For example, if the mold was detected in the jar stage, put the rest of the product back to the bag stage for awhile (after removing the contaminated product from the batch). If the mold is detected in the bag stage, hang the bud from string. If problems with mold occur prior to this, a dehumidifier in the drying room may be the answer. Aside from watching and smelling for mold, always remember to keep the product in the dark.

Ready to Smoke

A bud is completely dry, cured, and ready for consumption when the stem in the middle of the bud snaps when the bud is cracked with the fingers. The snap is easy to detect with practice. It is at this stage that the product can safely be sealed and stored for an indefinite period of time.

The longer you can stretch out this process, while also avoiding mold, the better. A typical dry and cure should take six to eight weeks from harvest to the finished product. Every time you open the jars you will be able to detect the fragrance of the product becoming more and more desirable as time progresses.

Chapter 15

Plant Stress and Pests

• •

In This Chapter

▶ Preventing over and under watering

▶ Identifying and understanding nutrient deficiencies

▶ Preventing plant diseases

▶ Dealing with plant infestations

• •

Even well-planned indoor gardens run into problems from time to time. A lot of problems are foreseeable or avoidable, but often they are sudden, unexpected, and potentially devastating. Luckily, marijuana is a resilient plant and has the ability to bounce back from trauma inflicted by insects, nutrient lockout, and some diseases. The key is to know what to look for and know how to treat it before it ruins your entire harvest.

If you've carefully followed the methods and recommendations in this book, you are likely to avoid the most obvious problems. However, just when you think your grow room is ticking along perfectly, you find mold on your buds, insect bites on the leaves or worse. Instead of freaking out and ripping out your plants or doing nothing and hoping the problem will solve itself, identify your problem in this chapter and treat it accordingly.

Each stress or disease or infestation has it's own line of treatment. Misdiagnosing the problem and treating your plants for a problem it doesn't have can lead to the complete destruction of your entire harvest. For instance, if you treat your plants for over watering, but they are actually suffering from nutrient lockout, they will eventually whither and die from both under watering and/or from the lack of one or more nutrients due to inappropriate pH levels.

Plant Stress

The key word for this section is "stress." While damage can be difficult to undo, stress can be relieved. In order to stop your plants from being stressed to the point where damage occurs, you must keep an eye out for all of the potential problems that you can unknowingly inflict on your plants.

Watering and Nutrients

How much and how often your plants are fed is a critical issue in any growing situation, indoor or out. When growing hydroponically, it's even more important as any miscalculations can quickly affect your crop and you could find yourself waking up to severely stunted plants. Fortunately, these problems are preventable as long as you monitor your feeding schedule and nutrient strength and adjust according to your plants' needs.

Over watering

The single, biggest mistake most beginning growers make is over watering their plants. Roots need to breathe and plants can be killed if their roots are kept too wet. In fact, plants seem to grow fastest when their roots are relatively dry, but not overly dry.

Moisture not absorbed rapidly by roots can soon turn stagnant. The plant quickly uses up any oxygen within the water, then is unable to respire further, resulting in a grow medium that's low in oxygen. Root rot (Pythium) thrives in low-oxygen conditions. Check to see if your medium is dry or wet before you water (or your pump comes on). If your medium is still wet on top, then you are over watering and need to water less often.

Just remember, plants grown hydroponically can yield marvelously, but since you are substituting for Mother Nature when you grow indoors, you must watch and care for your plants very carefully. When using hydroponics, you can have beautiful plants one day and near death the next. With the exception of lighting, using a light touch when administering water, nutrients, and everything else your plant requires is the way to go.

Low nutrient strength

Plants that don't acquire the necessary amounts of nutrients to sustain high growth rates, the nutrient flow reverses, causing the plants to weaken and wilt. Nutrient strength is also related to light intensity—plants under fluorescent lights usually require a lower nutrient concentration than those under HIDs.

Low nutrient strength isn't typically a problem with hydroponic growing unless you simply forgot to add nutrients to the reservoir. If you do suspect this is as the problem, make sure you check and re-check the PPM and pH levels, before adding any nutrients.

Nutrient deficiencies

Nutrient deficiencies in modern hydroponic gardens are rare. What most people see as a nutrient deficiency is usually a pH problem. pH that is too high or too low "locks out" your plants' ability to uptake nutrients. Since the plant can not uptake those nutrients, they appear to be deficient. In fact, there are probably plenty of nutrients in the solution but, due to pH lock-out, they are unavailable to the plant.

Adding supplements or more nutrients (which is what most people do) will only compound this problem by throwing the pH off even more and further raising the nutrient PPM. The best thing to do if you suspect any form of nutrient deficiency is to first check and adjust the pH as necessary. The proper pH range for your nutrient solution is between 5.5 and 6.5

Root problems

Root bound is caused by the roots of your plant outgrowing the container they are in. Plants that are root bound exhibit stunted growth, stretching, smaller and slower bud production, nutrient burn, or simple wilting. A root bound plant will always start yellowing with the bottom leaves and work its way up the plant until all the fan leaves are gone.

Since you are growing hydroponically, your options are limited to transplanting the plants to larger containers or immediately initiating flowering. Transplanting can be difficult to impossible depending on the system you are using. Initiating flowering will only begin to slow the plant's growth. The best solution to this problem is to avoid it altogether by keeping your plants to the height recommended for your hydroponics system.

Leaf Problems

Before trying to treat any leaf problems, always check the pH before increasing the nutrient strength. In the last few weeks of flowering a yellowing of the leaves is completely normal as the plant uses up all stored nutrients.

Yellowing (Chlorosis)

Chlorosis is a yellowing of leaf tissue due to a lack of chlorophyll. Possible causes of chlorosis include poor drainage, damaged roots, compacted roots, high pH levels, and nutrient deficiencies. Nutrient deficiencies may occur because there is an insufficient amount in the solution, but usually because the nutrients are unavailable to the plant due to a high pH level.

Yellowing in lower to middle leaves

Yellowing of the lower leaves/older growth is a sign of a possible nitrogen (N) deficiency. Nitrogen is a transferable element (the plant can move it around where needed). If a plant is not receiving enough nitrogen through the roots, it will transfer it from older growth. Plants that are nitrogen deficient will exhibit a lack of vigor and grow slowly, resulting in a weak and stunted plant that is significantly reduced in quality and yield. In a hydroponic system, usually the pH is too high and has locked out the available nitrogen.

Yellowing in upper leaves (New Growth)

Yellowing of new growth in the plants could be a sign of a sulphur (S) deficiency. Sulphur deficiency is pretty rare but usually starts off as a yellowing of the entire "younger" leaves, including the veins. Other signs of sulfur deficiency are elongated roots, woody stems, and leaf tips curling downward. However, most yellowing of the upper leaves occurs from bleaching, caused by the plant tops being too close to the HID lights. Put your hand between the plants and the light and if your hand gets too hot to hold it there, you should raise the lamp.

Leaf Curling

Leaves curling up can be a sign of a magnesium (Mg) deficiency caused by too low of a pH level. Magnesium deficiency will show as a yellowing (which may turn brown and crispy) and interveinal (in between the veins) yellowing beginning in the older leaves. Interveinal chlorosis (yellowing) will start at the leaf tip and progressing inward between the veins. It could also be a sign of excess heat and humidity in the grow room.

Leaves that curl under and burn at the tips and margins is usually a sign that the nutrient level is too high. Check and adjust the pH level as necessary and flush and decrease the nutrient level if necessary.

Stem Problems

From time to time every grower has accidentally broken a stem or eventually will. Stem breaks can come from a number of things: training, fallen lamp, inspecting. No matter how it happened the most important thing is to not panic. Marijuana plants have a great ability to bounce back even after a stem break.

A broken stem is usually not difficult to fix. Splint the stem with a popsicle stick or similar, then securely tape it to the stem at the break. Give your plant a week or so before inspecting the wound and by then regular growth should continue. If you've snapped the plant in half and it's barely hanging together, it's a goner, and you'll learn to be more careful next time.

Plant Diseases

Plant diseases are of an entirely different order than mere plant stress due to nutrient deficiencies or over watering. In fact, even a pest infestation can be overcome and you can eventually get your plant back to health. However, if your plants or a part of your plants has a disease you must act very quickly to isolate everything that is infected

Grey Mold (Botrytis)

Botrytis infections are found in humid grow rooms with a lack of proper ventilation. Look for masses of silver-gray spores on infected plant parts that are the furthest from the ventilation ducts. Black, shiny specks might also be seen embedded in diseased plant tissue, which allow the fungus to survive cold temperatures. Botrytis blight can affect leaves, stems, flowers, buds, seeds, seedlings and just about any other part of a plant with the exception of the roots.

The best way to manage this disease is by inspection, sanitation, and humidity reduction. Remove any and all infected flowers, leaves, or the entire plant if it's infected at the base. Take the moldy pieces far away from your grow area and get rid of them. If you start to notice any mold, immediately stop misting your plants until you can work out the problem.

To help eliminate the problem from occurring again, examine your air flow and circulation and make sure your plants are getting enough fresh air. Ventilate your grow space to prevent high humidity conditions. Even lowering the humidity slightly can have a significant effect on Botrytis. This is the most important means of stopping this fungus.

Added protection is available for many crops by applying a fungicide or combination of fungicides. However, Botrytis can develop resistance to certain chemicals. An ozone treatment is also an option, ozone is excellent for decimating spore counts in the grow room and a decent UV tube unit placed high in the room, with a fan blowing through it, can dramatically reduce the risk of Botrytis.

Root Rot (Pythium)

If the reservoir is heavily contaminated with debris, Pythium can develop and spread to a large number of plants very quickly. If the fungus infests a cutting bed or if contaminated water is used in propagation, large losses usually occur.

Almost all plants are susceptible to Pythium. Root tips, which are very important in taking up nutrients and water, are attacked and killed. Pythium also can rot the base of unrooted cuttings. Symptoms of Pythium include stunted plants, brown or dead root tips, and yellowing of the plants.

Pythium root rot is difficult to control once it has begun. Every effort should be directed toward preventing the disease before it begins. Cover your reservoir and disinfect all surfaces, tools, and equipment that will contact the nutrient solution. If that doesn't solve the problem, consider using hydrogen peroxide to clean your entire reservoir out, including the plant containers, if possible.

Plant Pests

While many different types of insects and animals can destroy or infest an outdoor grow, the number of pests that can harm an indoor grow is actually quite small. The biggest problems to affect an indoor crop are usually the result of grower action or inaction.

However, you should still keep a close eye on your plants and always keep a lookout for signs on an infestation. The faster you identify a pest problem, the faster you can eradicate it and help get your plants back into recovery-mode. The following section describes the types of pests that attack indoor grow rooms, how to identify them and finally have to get rid of them.

Domestic Pests

Sometimes the pests that can do the most damage to your plants aren't really pests at all, but your own dog, cat, ferret, or any other family pet running around your home. Just one of these animals can wipe our your entire crop in a single afternoon if allowed to sneak into your grow room.

Cats are especially curious and equally destructive as they play with, slash, and chew up your leaves. Puppies also like to use the stems to break their teeth in on. Any outdoor/indoor animal can also bring outdoor pests inside and transfer them from their fur to your grow room.

Prevention is the best way to deal with your own pets. They can do a lot of damage in very little time, so make that they can in no way access your grow room. If they have already destroyed some plants, you'll quickly learn your lesson and figure out how to keep them out permanently.

Spider Mites

Spider mites are very tiny—usually less than 1/50 inch (0.4mm) long as adults. They have four pairs of legs, no antennae and a single, oval body. Most also have the ability to produce a fine silk webbing, which is what you may notice before actually identifying these little pests.

Spider mites have tiny mouthparts that can pierce individual plant cells and remove the contents. This results in tiny yellow or white speckles on leaves. When many of these feeding spots occur near each other, the leaves take on a yellow or bronzed cast.

Figure 15-1:
Mites are one of the worst pests you can encounter while growing.

Signs of an infestation

Mites will first be noticed by the presence of small, discolored spots located near veins in the leaves. They may also coat leaves with a fine silk which collects dust and looks dirty. To see them, you might need the help of a 10x loupe or a 30x microscope. Mites will slow growth and attack the buds in advanced stages. The life cycle of the spider mite is closely tied to the temperature of the grow room, the more heat, the more mites.

Eliminating Spider Mites

Early detection of spider mites, before damage is noticed, is very important. The tiny spider mites can be detected only by a full and thorough leaf inspection (on both sides of the leaf). If you find spider mites, you must act fast and hit them hard with a bleach solution (1 tablespoon of bleach to 1 gallon of 95°F, pH balanced water) applied through a spray bottle.

Thrips

Thrips are small, fast-moving insects with wings. They rasp the marijuana leaves open and suck the sap out. Thrips prefer flowering tops and fresh, young leaves. Affected leaves have shiny, silvery spots. This is caused by the thrips sucking the chlorophyll out of the leaves. In spite of the fact that they're small, you can see them marching in columns on an infested plant.

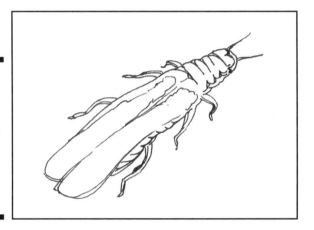

Figure 15-2:
Larvae and adults feed on stems, leaves and buds, using their piercing-sucking mouthparts.

Signs of an infestation

Thrips feed on new plant leaves, causing fresh leaf growth to deform. A metallic sheen on leaves is one sure indicator of thrips. Thrip feces is easy to see with the naked eye; they show up as black spots on the leaves and stems of infected areas. Thrips themselves are a pale pinkish color.

Eliminating Thrips

Cooler temperatures will slow down the life cycle and insect strips will trap adults. You can siphon them off by rustling the plant, and sucking them up with a vacuum hose. Fine powdered sulphur applied to the leaves will control them as well. Spraying the leaves with chrysanthemum also kills thrips.

Whiteflies

The whitefly life cycle is interesting in that the larval stage does all the damage. The larva will hatch and remain until it has quickly molted three times. Then it pupates and an adult emerges. White flies behave just like spider mites. The insect hides underneath the leaf and sucks it's dinner from it, which results in white spots on the top side of the leaf.

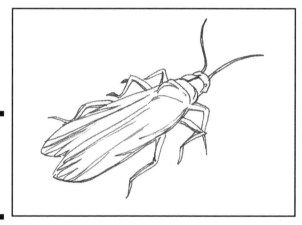

Figure 15-3:
Clouds of whiteflies fly up from foliage when disturbed.

Signs of an infestation

The top surface of leaves on infested plants become pale or spotted due to these insects feeding on the undersides of the leaves. White flies are easily spotted with the naked eye. Heavily infested plants will produce a buzzing cloud of flies if shaken. They looks like little white moths and are around two millimeters in size.

Controlling the Whitefly

Insecticidal soap will take care of an infestation, as will the more toxic insecticides. Apply the soap (plus a wetting agent) to every part of the plant, including both sides of the leaves. This will act to block the breathing pores and suffocate the pests.

Fungus Gnats

Fungus gnats are tiny black flies that are attracted to soils that are rich in compost and nutrients. They lay eggs on the surface, hatching into larvae. Those larvae feed on the root tissue, including root hairs, and the outer cell covering of the root; often leaving only the central tube of the root.

Figure 15-4: Fungus gnats often run across the growing medium and may fly if the plant is shaken.

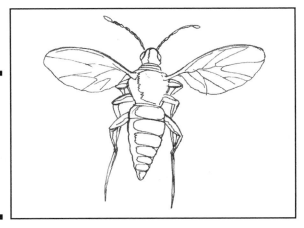

Signs of an infestation

External signs include discolored leaves and systemic plant failure. Fungus gnat adults will often run across the medium and may fly if the plant is shaken.

Controlling Fungus Gnats

Pyrethrum aerosols, as well as placing yellow sticky traps all around the plant, will help control the emerging adults. Gnatrol (containing natural Bt) is highly recommended.

Index

∙ ∙

A

Acidic 124–125
Activated carbon filters 164–166
  maintenance 166
  placement 165–166
Advanced techniques
  splitting leaves 203
  twisting and cracking 202–203
Aeroponics 109–110
Air
  temperature 124
Airflow 90–92
  exhaust 92
  intake 91
  oscillating fans 92
    placing 148
Air intake 91, 92–95
  ducting 94–95
  fans 93–94
  vents 93, 167
Alkaline 124–125

B

Ballasts 61–63
  switchable 62
Budsites 196, 198
Bulbs 60, 61–63
  comparison 54–55
  conversion 58–59
  replacing 62–63
Burn 186

C

C02 89, 132
Carbon Dioxide
  how plants use 89

Carbon dioxide 17, 18
Chlorophyll 20
Chlorosis 272
Clay pellets 117
Clones 171
  cutting 235
  foliar feeding 239
  from a flowing plant 228
  labeling 234
  maintenance 237
  potency 226
  providing nutrients for 239
  root development 238
  scraping 236
  selecting 233–234
  to determine sex 226–227
  transplanting 240–241
  troubleshooting 240
Cloning
  best time for 234
  equipment 229–231
  preparing medium for 232
  preparing mothers for 231–232
  setting up equipment for 233
  step by step 231–240
Coconut fiber 118
Conversion bulbs 58–59
Curing
  step by step 264–266

D

Dark period 196, 234–235
Diseases 273
Dissolved oxygen 124
Dissolved solids. *See* Parts per million
  (PPM)
Drying 262–264

quick method 263–264
Ducting 61, 94–95, 96–98
  noise 168

E
Electrical equipment
  grounding 145–146
  safety 145–146
Embryo 20
Exhaust fan
  choosing 97
  installing 97–98
Exhaust fans 96–98

F
Fans
  configuring 148–149
  noise 168
Female
  pre-flowers 203
Female plant 8–9
Fertilization 8
Floor
  protecting 147
Florescent 195
Flourescent lighting 231
Flowering 23, 175–180
  force 193
  initiating 205
  phase length 205
Flowering phase
  light cycle 245, 250
  lighting 244–245
  nutrients 244
  pruning during 247
Fluorescent 186
Fluorescent bulbs 65–67
  color spectrums 66–67
  hanging 152–153
Flushing 248–249
Foliar feeding
  clones 239

Fungus gnats 279

G
Germination 20, 179, 183–184
Growing media 114–119
  clay pellets 117–118
  coconut fiber 118
  maintenance 119
  rockwool 115–117
    advantages 116–117
    disadvantages 117
  soiless mix 118–119
  water culture 119
Growing medium
  preparing for cloning 232–233
Growing mediums
  moisture 139
    measuring 139
Growing techniques
  advanced 38
    screen of green 40
    sea of green 38
Grow room
  choosing 34, 43
    attics 35
    basements 35
    bedrooms 35
    closets 35
  concealing 166–170
  costs 50
  creating a plan 48–50
  enclosing 144–145
  locking 160
  planning 44–50
  preparing 144–145
  protecting 160–161
  security 41
  typical locations 35–36

H
Harvesting
  determine peak 249–252

quick cut 258
Hash 205, 261–262
Heating mat 231, 233
Heating pad 185
Hermaphrodite 8
Hermaphrodites 204–205
High-Pressure Sodium (HPS) 17
High Intensity Discharge (HID) 17,
    186, 272
High Intensity Discharge (HID) lamps
    271
  definition 54
  safety 54, 65
High Pressure Sodium (HPS) 54–55,
    57, 195, 245
  enhanced performance bulb 57
Hoods 61, 64
  air cooled 64
  dual fixture 64
Humidity 102–103, 263
  for seedlings 103
  lowering 103
Humidity dome 186, 230, 238
Hybrids 173
Hydroponic
  definition 27
Hydroponics
  advantages 30
  disadvantages 31
  superior plant growth 29
Hydroponic systems
  aeroponic 109–110
  building 105
  choosing 105
  components 111–113
  drip 106–107
  ebb and flow 107–108
  maintenance 113–114
    monthly 114
    post harvest 114
  nutrient film technique 110–111

I
Indica 11, 172, 249–252
Infestation
  fungus gnats 279
  spider mites 276
  thrips 277
  white flies 278
Insects. *See* Infestation
Ionizers 162

L
Leaves
  curling 273
  yellowing 272
Light cycle 55, 205
  day length 196
  for flowering 245–246
  night length 245
Lighting
  hanging 148–149
    horizontal 150
    vertical 150–153
  leaks 166–167
  optimum wattage 56
Light leaks 246

M
Male
  pre-flowers 204
Male plant 8–9
Manicuring 256
  cleanup 261–262
  step by step 259–262
Marijuana
  elements of growth 15–19
  potency 174–175
  varieties 9–11, 172–173
    hybrids 173
    indica 172
    sativa 172
  yield 175
Metal Halide 54–55, 58

super horizontal 58
Metal Halide (MH) 17, 195
Microscope 9, 251
Mold 266, 274–275
Mother plants 171, 225, 227–229,
    234–235
  choosing 228–229
  preparing for cloning 231
Mutations 226

N

N-P-K 244
Node 196, 198–199, 202, 204
NPK 133–135, 194
Nurtient lockout 123, 271
  repair 123
Nutrient Film Technique (NFT) 105,
    106
Nutrients 187
  basics 131–132
  burn 137, 194
  flowering 244
  how plants use 121
  labeing 132–134
  macro 132
  measuring 137–138
  micro 132
  multi-part 134, 194
  strength 136–138
    vegetative 194

O

Oasis cubes 185–190
Odor 161–163
  control
    ionizers 162
    ozone generators 162–164. *See
      also* Ozone generators
Oscillating fans 95–96
Osmosis 122
  reverse 122
Overfeeding 137

Over watering 129
Ozone generators 162–164
  maintenance 164
  placement 163–164
  safety 163

P

Parts per million (PPM) 137, 271
  meters 137
Pets 275
pH 248
pH level 124–129, 271–272
  metering 124–125
  optimal 125
pH meters 126–129
  adjustment 128–129
  constant 127
  maintenance 128
  portable 126
  strips 127
  test kit 127
  waterproof 126
Photoperiod 14–15, 19
Photosynthesis 13, 16, 18, 53, 89–90,
    193
Plant size
  planning 36
Pollen 8
Potency 198
Pre-flowers
  indentification 203–205
Preflowers 22
Protective glass 61
Pruning 196–197
  while flowering 247
Pythium. *See* Root rot

R

Reflective hoods
  horizontal 63
  vertical 63
Reflective light 67–70

reflectance rating 67, 236, 237
  wall coverings 67–70
    cleaning 69–70
Reflectors 60, 63–64
  horizontal 63
  vertical 63
Reservoir 111
Reservoirs
  maintenance 139–140
Respiration 14, 89
Rockwool
  starter cubes 185–190
Root bound 271
Rooting gel 231, 237
Root rot 270, 274–275
Roots 16
  temperature 124
Rubbing alcohol 231, 233, 256–257, 262
Ruderalis 11

S

Safety
  electrical 145–153
Sativa 10, 172, 249–252
Screen of green 38, 40
Screen of Green (ScrOG) 201
Sea of green 38
Sea of Green (SOG) 105, 241
Security
  buying equipment 157–159
  fan noise 168
  floor protection 147
  moving equipment 159
  odor. See Odor control
  rules 156
  trash removal 160–161
Seed banks
  choosing 179–182
  problems with 181
Seedling 21
Seedlings
  humidity 103

lighting 70, 186
nutrients 187
trays 186, 187
Seeds
  aquiring 172
  germinating. See Germination
  legalities 182
  ordering 180–181
  storing 182–183
  using bag 179
Seed set 8, 24
Sexual reproduction 171
Soil
  disadvantages to using 27
Soiless mix 118–119
Spider mites 276
Starter cubes 233, 235, 237, 239, 240
Stems
  bending 189
  repairing 273
Strains 172–179
  characteristics of 173–175
  top ten 176–178
Stress
  bending 202
  broken stems 273
  clones 240
  diseases 233, 273–274
  nutrient deficiency 271–273
  over-pruning 197
  overfeeding 195
  over watiner 270

T

Temperature 98–102
  extreme 100
  lowering 101
  maintaining 100
  measuring 99–103
  raising 101–102
  water 124
THC 8–11, 243, 251–252, 255, 263
Thinning 199–200

Thrips 277
Timers 112
Topping 198–199
Topping off 139, 139–140
Training 201–202, 246–247
Transplanting 185–190, 271
  equipment 185–187
  step-by-step 187–190
Trichomes 9, 248, 251, 252–253, 255
Tubing 112

U
Under watering 129

V
Vegetative Growth 21–22
Vegetative growth
  feeding regiment 195
  light cycle 196
  lighting 195–196
  nutrients 194
Vents 61

W
Wall covering
  hanging 146–147
Water
  evaporation 188
  functions 121
  quality 123
  temperature 124
Watering
  over 129
  over watering 270
  under 129–130
Water pump 112
Watts per square foot (WPSF) 56
Whiteflies 278
Wilting
  clones 233, 235, 238